HAPPINESS IS A STOCK THAT DOUBLES IN A YEAR

happiness
is a stock that
doubles
in a year

BY IRA U. COBLEIGH

published by

BERNARD GEIS ASSOCIATES

distributed by

RANDOM HOUSE

©1967 BY IRA U. COBLEIGH

All rights reserved
under International and
Pan American Conventions.
Published by Bernard Geis Associates;
Distributed by
Random House, Incorporated,
in New York and
simultaneously in Canada
by Random House of
Canada, Limited.

Fourth Printing

Charts on pages 45, 46, 47
prepared by R. W. Mansfield Co.
reproduced with their permission.
Charts on pages 51, 52, 53
prepared by Chartcraft, Inc.
reproduced with their permission.

author's
note

There are dozens of stocks mentioned, referred
to, or briefly described in this book. Information
respecting them was taken from sources considered reliable but in no way guaranteed. Moreover, the data concerning any individual issue
was necessarily prepared some months ago. Accordingly, if the reader is interested in any of
the stocks mentioned for possible purchase, sale,
or retention, it is essential that he acquire the

latest and most authoritative information about it before making any investment decision. This information should be secured from a responsible broker, dealer, investment adviser, financial publication, or service. In no event is any recommendation or endorsement made of any stock; and nothing herein is to be considered under any circumstance as an offer or inducement to buy, sell, or hold any security at any time.

IRA U. COBLEIGH

contents

**HAPPINESS
IS A STOCK THAT
DOUBLES
IN A YEAR**

prelude
to profitable
speculation

The stock market is a many-splendored thing. It's excitement, it's zest, it's a blending of high hopes and forlorn fears. It animates the lives of the 22 million Americans who now own stocks; and interest in Wall Street has become almost as traditional as apple pie, baseball, and motherhood. The stock market ranks third (after weather and health) as a topic of conversation.

MOTIVATION

Why do you, or should you, buy stocks? The
motives are many. You buy stocks because it's
the smart thing to do; to build a "second income"
from dividends on a list of blue chips; to increase
your worth or even make a fortune through owning
growth stocks — which reward you by increasing
their earnings, dividends, and market values
steadily over the years. You buy General Motors
because you own a Chevy, or you buy AT&T because you're a steady gabber on the phone. Or
you buy a particular stock not because you know
much about it but because you hope it will go up
so you can sell at a fat profit.

Also, you're attracted to "the market" by the
stories you hear — about somebody who put $1,000
in Xerox common in 1950 and now it's worth
$500,000 in market value. Or a neighbor who took
a flier in Valley Metallurgical and it went from 16
to over 100 in a single year! We all yearn to make
a lot of money in the market so that we can gaily
afford the visible trappings of opulence — minks,
mansions, Mercedeses, and Mediterranean
cruises! Cleaning up in the market is presumed
evidence of your success, sagacity, and merit.
It's fun, too, at a cocktail or dinner party to refer
casually to the big "score" you made in Fairchild
Camera; or to your shrewd purchase of Bristol-
Myers a few years back at $5 a share. Success in
stocks is good for the ego as well as the bank account.

But the stock market is no one-way street. While
it is true that you can make a killing ($20,000 and

up) and/or a fortune ($200,000 and up) in stocks, you can also lose your shirt! Between 1929 and 1933, the stock market sold off 89 percent; it declined over 25 percent in 1962, and around 21 percent between February and September of 1966. Individual stocks can dive dismally and without notice. Technicolor sold at 100 in 1930 and at $1 a year later. In 1966, Associated Oil & Gas plunged from 8 ¾ to 1 ¾ , and Far Western Financial from 13½ to 5. No matter how well you pick your stocks, they can vary in price widely in a single year; and if you want to make money, you must steel yourself against panicking when your stocks sell off a little or a lot. Because they surely will!

Actually, stockholders are divided into two major groups — investors and speculators. The investors generally buy and hold stocks of better quality for dividend income and long-term growth in value. That fellow who put $1,000 into Xerox in 1950 and still holds the stock (split several times since), now that it's worth half a million, is an investor! (Incidentally, don't you think if you'd bought Xerox seventeen years ago at $1,000, you might have been tempted to sell it for $10,000 or $50,000 or $100,000 on the way up?)

However, this book was not written for investors but for *speculators*. A speculator is not interested in holding a stock forever. He wants to buy today and sell at a profit tomorrow. Speculators seek action, animation, and early profits.

Probably there are at least 6 million Americans who are dyed-in-the-wool stock speculators. They love to buy and sell. They study charts, short-term swings, Dow-Jones theory, and follow the stocks that trade in big volume each day. They insist on being "where the action is"; and if a stock doesn't move after they've held it a while, they dump it and look around for another that will perform with more animation. Speculators have one aim in common — quick profits. Pin them down as to their real reason for buying a certain stock and a frequent reply will be: "I think it will double in a year or so."

And that's how this book got started. Because so many traders hope and aim to double their money, we did some research. We found that dozens of stocks double each year; that in 1965, over 10 percent of all the stocks on the American Stock Exchange doubled. Accordingly, this idea of buying a stock that can gain 100 percent in a year is not a woolly pipe dream but a proved mathematical possibility.

Our next step was to analyze some of the stocks that doubled within twelve months, to distill, if possible, from their performance the elements that made them go up faster than the rest. We thought stocks that advanced spectacularly ought to possess many qualities in common; and that other issues with similar characteristics might logically be expected to double in due course. We are convinced that stocks that can double are always lurking in the market waiting to be recognized. Among the 4,100 issues listed on stock exchanges and the 30,000 or so issues that trade with some activity over the counter, there are dozens of delightful winners each year. Our task is to smoke them out.

Actually, this book is arranged in a quite logical progression. The first eleven chapters contain general information about the stock market and outline the requirements for successful speculation. These chapters also describe the Dow Theory and several accepted methods for selection of stocks with above-average potentials for market gain.

Chapter 12 tabulates those stocks listed on the New York Stock Exchange and American Stock Exchange that doubled in the years 1961-64. Some comment is included on outstanding individual performers, and the thesis of this book is unfolded—that a large number of stocks do actually double in every bull-market year, and that there should be some way of screening and selecting probable winners in advance.

The third section, Chapters 13 and 14, reveals the listed stocks that doubled in 1965 and 1966. These years are singled out because they are the most recent, and the results permit comparison of 1965, a bull year, with 1966, when the market, as a whole, declined between February and December. This section points up the vital importance of timing for success in speculation. It also develops the logic of this book, which insists that stocks that double in any year have in common many recognizable and essential characteristics.

The final section, Chapters 15 through 20, is the most exciting part of the book. Here is the distillation of all the ideas presented earlier. It comes right out with a selected group of stocks, screened from hundreds of active market issues, believed to have outstanding potentials for market gain in 1967. Now, there is absolutely no warranty or assurance about the performance of these stocks. If all were to double in 1967, it would be miraculous; if quite a few doubled, it would be sensational; and great gain in any or all will depend importantly on a massive unpredictable — the market itself. If 1967 turns out to be a bull year, then these selections will plainly have a better chance to live up to their billings.

It should be clearly understood that these stocks are not tips or recommendations. They are issues selected because they seem to have basic qualities or characteristics similar to many of the stocks that have doubled in past years. If certain inbred and discernible qualities in a racehorse can make him a winner, perhaps selection on the basis of special characteristics can do the same thing for stocks.

Obviously, this is a bold and daring book because (1) such a small percentage of outstanding stocks double in any year, and (2) if anybody — banker, broker, baker, or busboy — knew for certain a stock that would double, he'd hock his shirt to buy it and wouldn't waste his time writing a book about it. The chances that any stock will double in a year are indeed mathematically small, but the endeavor to select and purchase issues that may perform in this manner adds excitement to life each passing day. America has always been a nation of risk-takers. All we've tried to do in this book is to narrow the element of risk.

This quest for bouncy stocks can add a constant zest to your life, fend off boredom, and, hopefully, make a lot of money for you. But there are no certainties or assurances. In a bear market, far fewer stocks will advance, even though they have a lot of things "going for them." Some stocks that should go up get stubborn and remain inert; and some stocks may soar like birds without apparent reason, simply because they have become "fashionable." In bull or bear markets, speculators will ever seek out these active stocks with potential for gain. This book is designed as a road map for such speculators, a partial guide for the bold, the sporting, and the cool — and even for us greedy ones for whom *happiness is a stock that doubles in a year.* Lots of luck and may all your stocks copy Xerox!

1
stock speculation for zest and gain

In 1924, Edgar Lawrence Smith's book *Common Stocks as Long Term Investments* was first published. It reoriented American investment thinking and helped launch a movement that has given character, acceptance, and stature to common stocks. It helped set in motion such a national enthusiasm for equities that today, forty-three years and one Great Depression later, there are 22 million stockholders in America, and common stocks have displaced bonds as the major holdings of many endowments and trust and pension funds. Mutual funds now own over $35 billion in common stocks; and $160 billion in the shares of major corporations (about one-third of outstanding shares listed on the New York Stock Exchange) are now held by institutions.

Indeed, a good common stock, although a flexible security type, is no longer regarded as a speculation or gamble but as a reliable long-term investment. Tens of thousands of individuals in all walks of life, by early investment in and patient retention of such stocks as IBM, General Motors, Minnesota Mining, Franklin Life, Republic National Life, Columbia Broadcasting, American Home Products, Northwest Airlines, McGraw-Hill, G. D. Searle, Xerox, and Litton Industries, have run a few thousand dollars into six- and seven-figure fortunes. This is quite wonderful, and all the experts agree that good common stocks as long-term holdings offer a practicable road to financial independence.

STOCKS FOR SPECULATION

Not everyone, however, is a patient long-term investor. For every two persons who buy and hold their stocks for years, there is one speculator — a person who wants action in his stocks, who gets a kick out of buying and selling and watching the ticker in board rooms, who seeks quick trading profits rather than dividend income or appreciation in his (or her) holdings over the years. If you have this zest for the market, this zeal to make money in a hurry, this yearning for swinging stocks and swift gains, then this book should prove of interest, and possibly of benefit, to you. Before you get involved in this exciting business of speculation, however, you should be cautioned on two points: (1) don't speculate with money you can't afford to lose — the rent money or the savings for retirement or a college education for Junior; and (2) be sure you have the right temperament and can accept losses as well as gains with equanimity.

The title *Happiness Is a Stock That Doubles in a Year* describes accurately the objective of this book. The great majority of stock traders hope to double their money; although in their impetuosity they often pull out early for a lesser gain. Larger rates of gain — 200 or 300 percent — are of course most acceptable, but the big accent is on speed and action. How fast can a given stock go up? Can it double in a year?

YOUR CHANCES OF DOUBLING YOUR MONEY

This goal of doubling your money is attractive to everybody, and especially so to persons in the upper tax brackets. For them, additional income may prove unrewarding if taxed at regular rates; and gains realized from successful trading in stocks held for six months or longer, taxable at only 25 percent, may significantly supplement regular income. But you don't have to be rich to enjoy the benefits of a 100 percent gain. It's rewarding to everybody!

If we agree that a twofold market gain is desirable and attractive, then the obvious question is: "What are our chances of attaining it?" Fairly good in some years; most difficult in others. For example, 1965 was a good speculative year. Fifty-five stocks listed on the New York Stock Exchange doubled in price; 104 issues on the American Stock Exchange doubled; and 315 issues actively traded in the over-the-counter (OTC) market also recorded gains of 100 percent or more. In other words, in 1965 there were 474 issues on the market which you could have bought at the beginning of the year and sold at a profit of 100 percent or more on the last business day of December; and this tabulation does not include speculations you might have made in Canadian markets, particularly on the Toronto Stock Exchange, far more volatile than any American mart. It is not uncommon for a Canadian oil or mining issue quoted in pennies to double in a week's time; or even, in some cases, overnight! Equally, however, rapid and even dizzy market descents are characteristics of certain Canadian markets, notably Toronto and the Canadian Stock Exchange in Montreal.

However, 1966 was not a typically conducive year for accomplishing the objective of this book. The figures are in a later chapter, but no one year should be taken as a criterion. After we have reviewed the results for the years 1961-66, I will give you my general analysis and forecast of the hopeful candidates for doubling in the year 1967.

We can logically conclude, however, that the idea of this book — doubling your money — is not a pipe dream but a distinct possibility. At least

6 million individuals in America today are active and avid speculators and traders. In fact, speculation in Wall Street has been increasingly popular since early 1964. A generation that has forgotten, or never read about, the Great Depression, and that was unfluttered by the 30 percent market decline in 1962, and took the $100 billion decline in the summer of 1966 in stride, remains ready and eager for speculative adventure — adventure that can provide a fascinating activity, with limitless variations and potentials, for a lifetime, and, if successful, can assure financial independence.

A broad survey taken among customers' brokers and based on dozens of visits to stock-exchange board rooms in many cities documents the fact that there are myriads of enthusiastic speculators and traders eager to learn about and to test any method or system that may direct them to fast-moving, swiftly profitable "performance" stocks.

There are indeed many valid approaches to the successful selection of speculative securities, and this book deals with a number of them. In fact, before any individual embarks on the daring venture of stock speculation, he should have some background about the market and the performance characteristics of different types of stocks, and some knowledge of fundamental and technical analysis of securities.

The strongest prevailing belief is that stocks in the long run will follow earnings. If the earnings go up, then the stocks will also rise. This, however, is a great oversimplification. There is often a time lag between the projection, or reporting, of higher earnings and a significant rise in the price of the stock. Not only that but earnings are valued differently in different market stages and in different industries. For example, stocks making up the Dow-Jones Industrial Average sold at 6 times earnings in the depths of the Great Depression, and at 24 times earnings in 1961. In 1966, Xerox sold at 55 times earnings at a time when General Motors was selling at 10 times earnings, Anaconda at 9, Florida Power & Light at 25, and Chase Manhattan Bank at 13.

The selection of securities on the basis of earnings is a basic element in the fundamental method of stock analysis, outlined in Chapter 2. The following chapters may broaden your knowledge of stock evaluation by specific coverage of Dow Theory, price/earnings multiples, theories about timing, and the use of bar and point-and-figure charts. Some of this you may find interesting and informative, but more impetuous readers will hasten on to the chapters listing stocks that have doubled, and in particular to the marshaling of candidates for market-doubling in 1967.

May we suggest, however, that to develop a better basis for selection and judgment of speculative stocks, you read rather carefully the pages on fundamental and technical methods, and learn to read the bar charts with reasonable skill, since so much investment literature is now devoted to the charting of stocks. Many expert traders insist that stocks are creatures of habit and will repeat at some future date a market performance recorded in the past. Hence the dedication to charts.

An important by-product of reading this book should be the development of your own market judgment; and it should be perfectly possible for you to make your own selections of "go" stocks on the basis of some of the valid techniques outlined later on. Speculation is still far more art than science, but knowledge of stock movements and the vital factors of demand and supply in any single issue should help you to succeed.

2

fundamental methods of stock evaluation

Our stated program is to search for undervalued stocks and to so time their purchase that we may realize target capital gains on them of 100 percent or more within the ensuing twelve months. Vital to success in such a program is a reliable method of valuation or appraisal that can indicate with some accuracy when a stock is undervalued in the marketplace and at what level it offers legitimate promise of a significant gain in price. By all means the oldest and most respected technique for analysis of stock values is the fundamental method.

THE BASIC INGREDIENTS

The fundamental approach centers around the axiom "Stock prices are the slaves of earning power." Over a period of time, stocks tend to rise quite faithfully in response to increases in earnings (and to decline when earnings slip).

If you doubt that, take a look at the recent earnings growth of such leaders as IBM, McGraw-Hill, Texas Instruments, Fairchild Camera, Polaroid, and Admiral. You will find, in every instance, a rate of growth in net earnings far above that of the average corporation; and that that rate of growth was translated into powerful upthrusts in the prices of the stocks.

The rise in stock prices in response to a favorable profit trend is seldom precisely parallel to it. Share prices in issues that have attracted an enthusiastic market following have in fact often risen at far steeper rates than the related earnings, on occasion reaching quite dazzling price/earnings multiples of 60 or more.

EARNINGS AS PROPELLANTS

A study of earning power is the backbone of the fundamental method of security appraisal. A rising long-term trend in earnings is an almost certain clue to a stock that will advance in the market. However, in some industries (cyclical ones such as building materials, copper, machine tools), earnings may rise rapidly for a time, only to fall off sharply, and it is most important to note when these changes in direction take place. Some companies will show reduced earnings in a year, due perhaps to large outlays for plant expansion or research of a new product. This also must be taken into account, because in the following year these capital investments may result in net earnings at an all-time high.

For example, some excellent electric-utility stocks and life-insurance-company shares recorded no significant price gains (and some actual declines) between 1964 and the summer of 1966, yet their earnings and dividends advanced during this period without a pause to new highs. These conservative or defensive-type investments simply failed, during the time span in question, to attract enthusiastic buying, not because their statistics were unfavorable — quite the contrary — but because the issues generated no market "oomph," and gain-minded traders preferred to purchase stocks that were (1) more active on the tape, (2) more glamorous (and speculative) in nature, and (3) in shorter supply. We conclude, therefore, that when rising earnings were insufficient market propellants, the issues were either (1) too high-priced earlier and stabilized at lower levels, (2) not sufficiently glamorous to attract a following of "swinging" speculators, or (3) awaiting a time when sound dividend-paying stocks again became fashionable among market operators.

Earnings are, moreover, a two-way street, and

if stocks go up when earnings rise, they also go down when earnings fall. (Example: American Motors in 1966, the savings-and-loan, and cement stocks in 1965-66.)

GROWTH FACTORS

Not only rising earnings but general growth in sales and assets as well are important fundamental factors influencing stock prices. Rates of growth are especially important. A company doubling its sales in five years, with a corresponding increase in net, will surely have a stock with a rising market trend. Companies whose sales and earnings have grown at such, or even better, rates have indeed attracted strong market followings. Examples of companies growing in this manner would include: Litton, American Hospital Supply, Northwest Airlines, Gulf & Western Industries, Occidental Petroleum, and Republic National Life.

THE MANAGEMENT FACTOR

We would not be covering fundamental methods of analysis at all well if we didn't say something about management. How many great companies do we know that are the lengthened shadows of enormously gifted and energized individuals? Can you imagine the Ford Motor Company without the pioneer genius of Henry Ford; Helena Rubinstein without the amazing skills of its founder; Litton Industries if "Tex" Thornton hadn't come along; IBM with the Watsons absent; Republic National Life without Theodore Beasley; Norfolk & Western without Mr. Saunders; Perkin-Elmer minus Richard Perkin? Of course, a big corporation today is not a one-man band, but it is important to note how many great companies have become industrial titans because of their leadership by individuals endowed with remarkable amounts of initiative, imagination, drive, and guts. Outstandingly competent business virtuosi are not always recognized in early corporate phases; and the big trend today is to run the show by management teams, with each member having considerable autonomy in his own department or division. Alfred Sloan's excellent book, *My Years with General Motors*, most effectively outlines the development of corporate efficiency under a team of division managers, with considerable interdivision competition.

Admittedly the qualities of good management are hard to define; but they are fairly easy to document. In general, quality management is evidenced by rising sales, introduction and marketing of new products or services, improving profit margins, and especially the *increase of profits* at a faster rate than sales. The ultimate test of management is the conversion of sales into net profits. Thus, in any given industry, look for the company with the best growth rate in gross income, the highest ratio of net profits to sales volume, and the highest returns on invested capital. These relationships will vary, of course, from industry to industry and company to com-

pany; and you can't compare statistical ratios
as between a railroad and a department store,
or an electronics company. But within any industry you can compare results, year by year,
and quarterly, and the best results at the cash
register are almost invariably reported by the
best managed companies.

OTHER FUNDAMENTAL FACTORS

While a study of earnings is the backbone of
security appraisal, there are many other fundamental factors that have an important bearing
on the thrust and direction of stock prices. These
include such items as balance-sheet positions
(current position and debt structure); a calculation and comparison of profit margins; percent-
ages earned on invested capital and on net worth
(stockholders' equity); cash flow; and dividend
payments. Further, a review of current and past
annual reports may prove revealing. Observation and cataloging of changes in sales, expenditures for research, development of new products
or services, and changes in dividend payments
will round out the valuation procedure.

Price/earnings multiples (see Chapter 3) are
usually significant, and comparisons of these
ratios with those of other companies in the same
industry are often useful.

The most successful companies will display
two important earnings characteristics: (1) their
net earnings will increase year by year (the
rapidly growing ones may increase their net profits 10 percent or more annually); and (2) their

earnings will grow at a faster rate than their sales. Seek out companies displaying these characteristics and you're quite likely to find shares with potentials for unusual market gain.

A high price/earnings multiple is often an index of outstanding quality or unusual growth potential or both (IBM, Xerox, Fairchild Camera, and Polaroid all sell consistently at multiples of 40 or higher). These ratios are, however, somewhat confusing because they're constantly changing. Generally, P/E ratios rise during bull markets and fall in bear ones; but if a company's earnings dive in a given year, the subject stock may actually sell at a substantially higher than normal multiple of (lower) per share earnings.

FUNDAMENTALS IN GENERAL

The fundamental approach to security values includes not only the analysis of industrial and corporate statistics outlined above but a consideration of prevailing political and economic conditions as well. Credit conditions and the supply and price (interest rate) of money are vital factors. In the early stages of bull markets, money is usually both plentiful and cheap. Companies borrow for corporate expansion, and individuals borrow increasingly to buy securities. New plant additions and expansions tend to increase corporate earnings, and stocks respond to the higher earning power by going up. It is in this early phase of a bull market, of course, that the most attractive purchasing opportunities in common stocks appear. However, in this stage (which often follows a period of recession), many investors either are timid because they are mindful of fairly recent market losses, or lack available funds for aggressive speculation. This tentative attitude toward the market fades as stocks advance, and as the incomes of individuals and corporations advance. The years 1960-66 powerfully illustrate the economic upsurge we have just described, which led to the next market stage, wherein money supply and credit availability played key roles. In February, 1966, the Federal Reserve rediscount rate was advanced from 4 to 4.5 percent, and in March, general interest rates reached the highest levels in forty years. Blue-chip stocks yielded only 60 percent of the income yields of high-grade corporate bonds; banks throughout the land were charging 6 percent and more on individual loans, and credit became progressively restrictive. This monetary situation had the predictable effect of slowing down stock buying, and the market sold off over 20 points on the Dow-Jones Industrial Average (DJIA) in the first week in May, 1966.

The stiffening of credit availability and rates (often accompanied by increased margin requirements) has historically tended to put a brake on market enthusiasm, and both credit and margins (treated in detail in Chapter 11) are basic elements in the fundamental analysis of securities.

FUNDAMENTAL VALIDITY

Most sophisticated investors (individual and institutional) agree that knowledge and appraisal of the fundamental factors we have cited provide vital guidelines to the selection of dynamic stocks. These fundamentals might be said to represent the logical factors bearing upon the evaluation of stocks, and are the basic tools of those who invest for sustained income and long-term growth. But changing psychology often has a greater bearing on the current stock quotations than statistical changes within a company or industry.

As long as America is a land of free enterprise, our stock market will continue a vast, vibrant auction center, a place where buyers and sellers of securities meet and exchange views on values. While the rise and fall of prices will ever be related to corporate earnings and dividends, it will also be subject to the ever-shifting attitudes, psychological whims, and caprices of the public.

So it is that, in our endeavor to winnow winners from some 34,000 different stock issues traded with some frequency in the listed and OTC markets, we must take into proper consideration both the impact of human emotions and corporate arithmetic in projecting the prices of shares. Stock prices can sometimes be as much slaves to emotions as to earning power.

In the chapters that follow, we shall explore a widely popular theory that the best guide to stock prices is the market itself; that in any final appraisal of a corporate share or of the whole market, the consensus provided by daily volume and price changes can direct us to the stocks that are on the road to stardom — and keep us away from the losers.

3
price/earnings multiples

As a guide to speculative values, a fundamental tool of security analysis that has gained wide acceptance, especially in the past twenty years, is the price/earnings multiple. Simply stated, this is the ratio that indicates, at a given point in time, how many dollars investors are willing to pay for a dollar of net earnings, either in a group of stocks such as the DJIA, or in an individual company share. This ratio is changing ceaselessly, both because net earnings themselves vary with each quarterly statement published and because investors and speculators are willing to pay a lot more for a given dollar of earnings at one market stage than at another. Further, these ratios vary noticeably from industry to industry, and from company to company. A good copper stock may sell at 11 times earnings, while a romance stock, like Xerox, may sell at 60 times earnings, and a representative utility at 25 times. There are no absolutes, but in each industry and stock an average ratio, calculated over a given ten-year period, may serve as a useful guideline.

By way of illustration, we are listing below the average price/earnings ratio for forty representative stocks in different investment fields:

10-YEAR AVERAGE P/E RATIOS — 1955-64

STOCK	AVERAGE MULTIPLE
Allis-Chalmers	19
International Harvester	12
Boeing	12
Douglas Aircraft	22
Pan American World Airways	13
United Airlines	14
General Motors	13
Chrysler	9
General Tire & Rubber	13
Goodyear Tire & Rubber	14
Alpha Portland Cement	8
Penn-Dixie Cement	11
Du Pont	25
Allied Chemical	15
Merck	27

STOCK	AVERAGE MULTIPLE
Parke, Davis	19
General Electric	27
Westinghouse Electric	24
General Foods	21
Standard Brands	17
Colgate-Palmolive	15
Procter & Gamble	23
Minnesota Mining	37
Polaroid	52
Aluminum Company of America	28
Reynolds Metals	23
Anaconda	10
Kennecott Copper	13
International Business Machines	37
National Cash Register	28
Standard Oil (N. J.)	16
Texaco	14
International Paper	19
St. Regis Paper	17
R. H. Macy	13
Federated Department Stores	17
U. S. Steel	15
Republic Steel	13
American Tobacco	12
Reynolds Tobacco	15

Just for practice, compare these ratios with those prevailing on the day you read this page.

The foregoing will give you food for thought on this subject of ratios. Why is a dollar of earnings in Merck always worth more than in Parke, Davis? in Polaroid, than in Minnesota Mining? in Du Pont, than in Allied Chemical? in IBM, than in National Cash Register?

There can also be some notable changes in P/E ratios over a period of time. For example, in 1961, good savings-and-loan stocks sold at 20 to 25 times earnings, against 6 times in the spring of 1966, after declining profits and rises in mortgage defaults had set in. On the other side of the coin, Coca-Cola Company, with a ten-year (1955-64) average multiple of 22 times, sold at 28 times in mid-1966; Texas Gulf Sulphur upgraded from 18 times to a historic 42; Admiral, from 18 to 31; while Honeywell sold quite consistently for twelve years in a row at a multiple of 29. When a stock gains an eager and enthusiastic market following, its price/earnings ratio seems certain to move ahead by several multiples. This is sort of a popularity rating and not necessarily earned by a corresponding rise in profitability.

RATIOS JUSTIFIED

A review of this subject of P/E ratios should be of help when it comes to searching out undervalued issues and shares that can double. It is to be observed that the leading stock in its industry usually commands the highest multiple, except in cases where younger or junior companies display an exceptional rate of growth. High P/E ratios are generally a tribute (1) to established investment quality and stature and/ or (2) to a sustained high growth rate, which evidences managerial initiative and competence. Rapidly rising P/E multiples occur frequently in the middle stages of powerful bull markets and in the cases of notably expanding companies in romantic industries — electronics, aerospace, automation, publishing, and the like.

However, in cyclical stocks (copper, machine tools, steels, etc.) the situation may be reversed. Here $1 of earnings may be worth $14 in the early phase of a bull market, $12 midway, and $8 just before a major recession or downturn (because there are then no expected rises in profits to discount, and per-share profits have reached a cyclical peak).

DJIA EARNINGS MULTIPLES

Wide consideration is given to the P/E multiples of the DJIA, because the ratios prevailing in this group, and changes in them, are thought to exert a pervasive influence over the ratios at which other, less renowned equities may sell. On Friday, May 6, 1966, the DJIA closed at 902.-83, which was 16.8 times the 1965 earnings per share of the group. This date was selected because it marked a breakthrough to the lowest DJIA multiple in ten years. Only when the DJIA plunged to 535.76 in June, 1962, did a comparable multiple exist. On the same date (May 6, 1966), Xerox sold at 74 times net earnings (for the most recently reported twelve-month period); Polaroid at 64; IBM at 39; General Motors at 12; and AT&T at 16.

This brings us to the key question: "What is normal?" For individual stocks we answered this by presenting a ten-year average. For the DJIA, "normal," between 1958 and 1964, averaged about 18 times.

In the spring of 1949, however, the ratio was only 7; in 1956, it advanced above 15 for the first time since the end of World War II; and in December, 1961, the DJIA multiple hit an all-time high of 25. What can we conclude from all this? That stocks are probably a buy when the DJIA dips below 15 times earnings; and certainly so if the multiple drops to 10.

Many analysts have reached the conclusion that, with such exceptions as Polaroid or Fairchild Camera, we have now entered a new era of lower multiples on the DJIA; and that 15 to 16 times rather than 18 times should now be regarded as normal. Why? Because we are reaching a ceiling on growth. In May, 1966, the plants of America were operating at 93 percent of capacity and unemployment was at a very low 3.7 percent. Whereas, in an earlier phase of the economy (1962), when plant capacity was only 85 percent occupied and unemployment stood at 6 percent, there was ample room for forward motion. Ninety-three percent represents close to maximum use of substantially greater production facilities than were in operation in 1962. Bull markets have always placed a premium on the expectation of national growth; and apparently this premium, as it relates to the DJIA, is a multiple of around 2 (the difference between 16 and 18 times).

Another theory advanced to justify a lower

multiple — around 16 — as normal is the depreciation factor. A stock that has in addition to its net earnings a high per-share percentage of depreciation is thought to be worth measurably more than a stock with lower "cash flow" from depreciation. This "cash flow," deriving from depreciation money retained by the company, has the same usefulness in corporate expansion as funds raised by borrowing or by sales of securities; and financing new capacity in this way builds solidly for higher earnings and dividends in future years. So it is entirely proper to accord a "plus" value to a stock with greater depreciation funds in back of net earnings after taxes. Unspent cash in the form of depreciation permits larger distribution of both immediate and future cash dividends.

This "cash flow" element expands most noticeably after a period of heavy additions to plant and equipment. Quite a few economists now feel that we will not continue to make corporate capital improvements at the same rate as we did from 1955 to 1962, and, therefore, we will not have another year like 1962, when corporate net profits and depreciation charges were just about equal ($31 billion versus $30 billion). We would expect, in the years till 1970, a situation where every dollar of net profit will be supplemented by no more than 55 cents in depreciation charges.

We have gone into some detail about this P/E business because it is so widely talked about and because a low multiple (historically) may properly be considered as a legitimate basis for regarding a security as underpriced — and possibly capable of doubling. We think we can set down a few helpful guidelines.

1. If the DJIA multiple is below 12, the whole market is probably in or near an attractive buying range.

2. Allow (and add) a multiple of at least 2 for a growth rate (in net) averaging better than 10 percent annually.

3. Allow a multiple of 2 for annual depreciation funds aggregating 70 percent or more of per share net.

As a "norm" for the DJIA, we think it safe to consider 16 times. Among individual industries and issues, however, comparison should be made of the current multiple, with the average one prevailing for the preceding five years (at least). If the current multiple is 25 percent lower than this average, then you may have unearthed an underpriced stock.

If two companies in the same field, such as Du Pont and Allied Chemical, have consistently displayed a wide divergence in P/E ratios, respect that difference! The high-quality issue is far more likely to retain or increase its lofty multiple than the secondary one is to move up to a higher ratio.

Clouds on an industrial horizon can lower traditional ratios. In the coal industry, for example, P/E ratios advanced during the 1950's, reflecting the growth in coal fueling of electric-power stations. Then, with the threat of atom-power generation, traditional coal-share P/E ratios dipped from 15 to around 10 in 1966.

Bear always in mind that P/E ratios are just another tool or bench mark useful in reaching a decision as to whether "the market," or a particular stock, is at a buy or a sell level. As a valuation cross check, ratios are splendid, but as a determining price factor, they're anything but sure fire. They may aim well but they seldom hit the bull's-eye.

4

technical analysis– a popular tool for avid speculators

Within the past decade, several million new stock speculators have entered Wall Street. Most of these are too young to remember the Great Depression, and they seem confidently to assume that, with the exception of a few short-lived flutters and downspins, the market will continue to go up indefinitely. This new "action" class of speculators is constantly searching for some new method or system "to beat the market." Traders of this ilk tend to view with disdain the funda-

mental approach — reliance on such ancient verities as earnings, profits, profit margins, dividends, growth rates, book value, and percentage
earned on equity. For the "quick buck" boys, the
guidance given, and the possible clues to underpriced stocks supplied by these fundamentals
are too languid and too inert. True, a given stock
with a powerful and visible uptrend in net earnings will probably advance over time; but it may
take a year or two before the public is sufficiently aware of this upthrust in earnings to
propel a major market gain. Moreover, in a market
selloff, such as summer, 1962, fundamentally
strong stocks with dynamic earnings went down
with the rest. Anyway, two years is far too long a
time for an impetuous speculator to wait. So the
itchy trader seeks a method of winnowing out
stocks that may shortly advance for reasons not
found in their earnings reports or dividend declarations. Many stocks go up just because they
have attracted a following and become fashionable.

TECHNICAL ANALYSIS

One of these acclaimed methods for perceiving
in advance the direction of stock prices is called
technical analysis. This attempts to study the
day-by-day performance of individual stocks, and
of the market as a whole, by careful analysis of
daily volumes of trading and price movements.
Technical analysis endeavors to discern, from
past performance of active individual stocks, or
of market averages such as the Dow-Jones In-

dustrial Average, the probable immediate future trends. The theory behind this is that market movements are quite as much psychological as logical phenomena. Often a stock will go up not because of any significant change in its fundamental values, but because a new and heavier flow of the public's money is entering the issue. This condition can be quite apparent when (1) the daily trading volume in the stock increases noticeably above average volume for the past 30 days, and (2) when this increase in volume is accompanied by higher price quotations and, especially, new "highs." Conversely, when volume increases above recent daily averages, with a *downtrend* in price, the message is given that the public is moving *out* of that issue; that its sale is indicated; and that a further price decline may be expected.

NEED FOR CHARTS

To observe, record, and analyze this price-and-volume data, charts are essential. It will be helpful to spend a little time on these charts before going on to their application and use as tools for making shrewd and timely market decisions either to buy or to sell.

BAR CHARTS

The most popular and best understood stock chart is called a bar chart. This type of chart may cover transactions for a day, a week, a month, or a year. Customarily, the horizontal scale, running from left to right, will be the time scale covering the period included; while the vertical scale will represent the price changes. If the chart is of ordinary squares, or cross-section paper, both the horizontal (time) scale and the vertical (price) scale will be uniform. The distance on the chart will be the same between a price of 10 and 20 as between 90 and 100.

Most market "pros," however, prefer a logarithmic or scale chart. Such a chart has a larger space or distance between prices at lower levels than at higher ones. The reason for using a chart scale that shrinks as prices rise is to bring price changes into perspective and to facilitate percentage comparisons. For example, if a stock moves from 10 to 20, it has gained 100 percent; but if it moves from 50 to 60 (also 10 points), it has gained but 20 percent. Since it's the percentage gain that is important, the "log" chart is superior, since each advance of, say, 10 percent will represent the same vertical distance on the chart whether the actual price movement is from 10 to 11 or from 100 to 110.

Plotting the chart is pretty well standardized. You connect the day's high and the day's low by a vertical line, and the closing price is shown by a very short horizontal line crossing the vertical one. You plot in the same data each succeeding day, and shortly you will have a chart that shows a trend — which is what we're really looking for.

About volume: that is usually shown on a special scale running along the bottom of the page; and many precise individuals also make

notes at the bottom indicating when stocks sell
ex dividend, ex rights, pay extra dividends, stock
dividends and so on. There is no sense, however,
in keeping charts unless they're up to date. If
you're going to plot the charts yourself, you
should be a neat, patient, and mathematically
minded individual. Otherwise, you should probably get the charts you want, on the issues that
interest you, from Dines Service, Trendline,
Mansfield, M. C. Horsey, or one of the other
services. Many investment services and market
letters of leading stock-exchange firms illustrate
market motion in individual stocks and in the
whole market by bar charts.

If you prefer doing the charts yourself, get
the proper equipment: the right pen or pencil,
a triangle, a ruler, folders for the charts; and have
a well-lighted table or desk at which to work.
Keep everybody (particularly children) away
from your desk so that your charts won't get
messed up. Finally, don't try to chart twenty
stocks a day. If you get behind, you'll be in a bind.
Try no more than four or five for openers. You
have a choice of time periods. A weekly or a
monthly chart is best for most speculators interested in detecting short- or intermediate-term
trends.

These charts do several things for you. First,
they give you the real story about the market —
what people were actually willing to pay or take
for a given stock on given days. This is the real
value of any stock — what it will fetch on the market. Emotion or mass psychology, rather than

reason, may have dictated the prices recorded, but they are genuine factors and, many feel, the best indicators of future trends. Your chart reveals what has been called "the bloodless verdict of the marketplace."

Very often a collection of these weekly or monthly charts placed together in order may reveal a strong directional trend. Particularly in the cases of companies whose earnings are rising steadily in each succeeding quarter, you may observe a line on the chart that follows a steady upward slope. It may not necessarily be an uptrend in earnings that provides the propulsion. The same upslant might result if the stock were steadily under accumulation for any cause.

EXAMPLES

BAR CHART—BAUSCH & LOMB, 1966

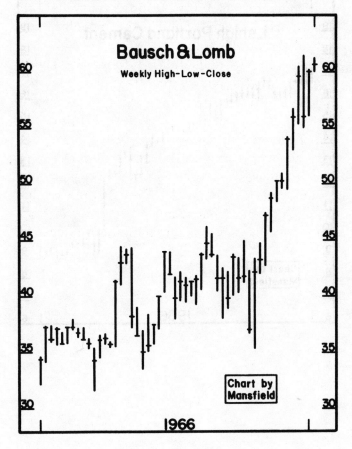

BAR CHART — LEHIGH PORTLAND
CEMENT, *1966*

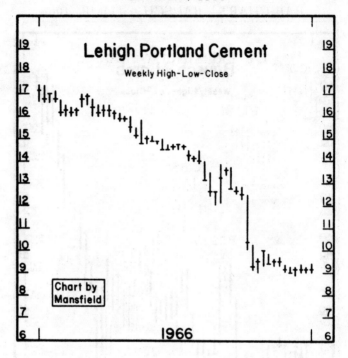

BAR CHART — DOW-JONES INDUSTRIAL AVERAGE, *1966*

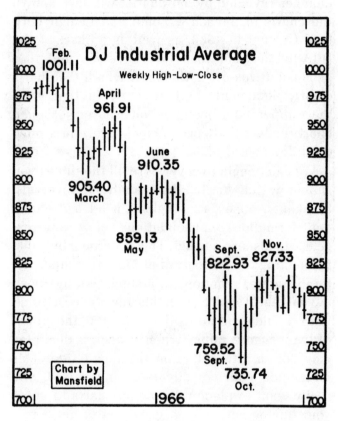

To illustrate the graphic account of market changes revealed by bar charts, we have shown the charts of Bausch & Lomb and Lehigh Portland Cement in 1966, as well as a chart of the DJIA for the year 1966. (We have selected 1966 because it was a volatile year, which the charts clearly document. In fact, early in that year, there appeared formations that assured seasoned chart readers that certain stocks were in a powerful downward phase.)

We can't begin to cover here all the things you should watch for in chart analysis: reversals, breakouts, boxes, rectangles, "head and shoulder" formations, consolidations, etc. Your real goal is to discern a trend. This is defined by a line connecting the bottoms of at least two (and preferably more) reactions in a stock that has·been advancing. In such a case, this line (called a trendline) should slant upward. Connecting the "tops" of two or more rallies when a stock is declining may define a trendline on the down side. This all sounds a bit complicated — and it is. If you really want to place reliance on charts to guide your buying and selling, you'd better get a professional book or two on the subject — possibly the one on *Technical Analysis* by Edwards and Magee. But from what we've given here, you should be able to look at a representative bar chart and derive some sort of message from it. The more you've learned about charts, the more distinct will be the message.

Most stocks perform erratically, surging to peaks, dropping back, then surging ahead again, with the pivot zones called support or resistance areas. Many pros are convinced that each stock develops its own unique pattern; and that trends recorded in the past may be expected to recur with considerable fidelity at a later date. From this historical perspective, traders often feel they can estimate with some accuracy how far up or down a stock will go in a given "move."

POINT-AND-FIGURE CHARTS

Another type of chart, used less frequently, is the point-and-figure chart. Here a uniform (not logarithmic) paper is used with each box or square representing a unit of price. Customarily, each square will represent one point in the price of a stock, although in shares selling below 20, each box may represent only 1/2 point. Price changes, to be recorded on the chart, must cover at least three squares up or down. The letter X is customarily used to denote up moves and O for down moves. Trendlines are not drawn until a bullish formation or a bearish formation has appeared. Then the trendline will be constructed quite arbitrarily at an angle of 45 degrees (either up or down). Stocks are thought to be in a buying range when actual sales are above the trendline; and in a selling phase when the trading takes place at prices below the trendline.

Point-and-figure charts do not concern themselves with a time factor. They simply record changes in price. What they aim to do is to reveal the supply-and-demand factors affecting a given stock. The theory is that if demand is strong (more powerful than supply), then the stock will continue to go up until supply (selling) is more insistent. Then the stock will decline. Key patterns on point-and-figure charts are triple-top and triple-bottom formations and bullish or bearish triangles.

Point-and-figure savants, after they have arrived at a reasonably well-marked trendline, often use a quite simple formula for "counting" the market to determine the probable immediate or intermediate price objective of a given stock. They count the number of squares (across) used in building the chart pattern, and multiply that by 3 (because it takes a move of at least three squares at a time to define a trend reversal). The product thus reached is, theoretically, the forthcoming nearby or intermediate price objective of the subject stock. This "count" will indicate the probable price the stock you've been watching should reach in a forthcoming rally, but it won't tell you *when* that price will be reached.

1966 POINT-AND-FIGURE CHART
Based on 11, 12, 1, 2 and closing prices
The Dow-Jones Industrial Average
(A 5 x 15 point Reversal Chart)

1966 POINT-AND-FIGURE CHART
Based on daily highs and lows
Lehigh Portland Cement Common
(½ x 1½ point Reversal Chart)

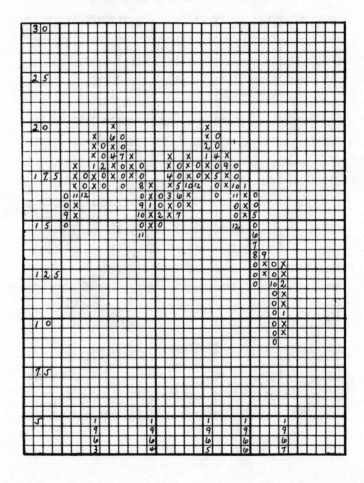

1966 POINT-AND-FIGURE CHART
Based on daily highs and lows
Bausch & Lomb Common
(½ x 1½ point Reversal Chart)

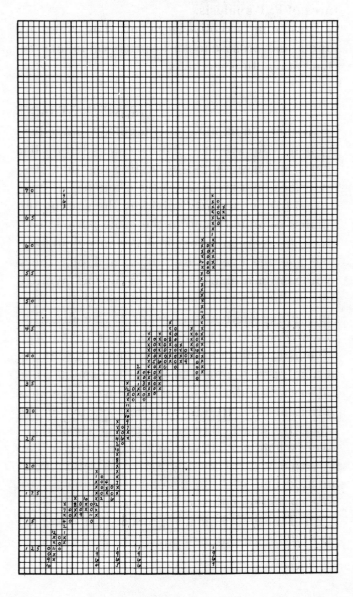

For delving into point-and-figure charts, Chart-craft, Inc. prepares charts in profusion on individual stocks each week; and they also can supply a booklet or brochure describing major features of P&F analysis.

These charts should be regarded as useful adjuncts and cross checks to price valuations arrived at by other methods.

MOVING AVERAGES

Another sophisticated technical procedure is the moving average. This is calculated on bar charts and is obtained by adding together closing prices on a given stock for a number of days (three, five, or ten) and dividing the sum by the number of units traded in the same period. This gives an average price; and if you calculate a new average every three days, and plot these averages on a chart, you get a moving average or trendline. In an active market period, this moving-average method will point to the direction in which stocks are moving, but it is less informative as to when the top or bottom of a swing is at hand; and is inconclusive in horizontal price patterns. Standard use relates moving averages to regular price trends, with both plotted on the same bar chart. Buying or selling signals are given when moving-average lines cross price-pattern lines. All this, however, is rather complicated and of little practical use unless you dote on mathematics and are a chart bug.

All of these technical approaches are designed (1) to define trendlines and (2) to give guidance for proper action by pointing the way to significant trend changes. But these systems, charts, volume studies, moving averages, and the rest depend in great part on the skill, judgment, and experience of the person who interprets the data. The mathematics may be right but the conclusions wrong!

Many active traders who on occasion get stocks that double, place great reliance on some form of technical analysis; but unless you are, or become, a gifted and hard-working chartist, you'll probably do just as well if you derive inspiration on market timing from other sources.

5

the dow theory

One of the oldest techniques of projection of stock prices is the renowned Dow Theory. It has rabid fans, lifelong devotees, and dedicated followers — and ardent detractors as well — all over the world. It can offer some interesting guidelines in the program of short-term speculation to which we are dedicated.

The Dow Theory did not come to life in an instant like Athena, springing full-grown from the head of Zeus, but represents a notable evolution of thought.

Charles H. Dow, its creator, was a member of
the New York Stock Exchange between December, 1885, and April 30, 1891, but is better
known as America's pioneer financial journalist,
a founder of Dow Jones & Company (1882), and
editor of *The Wall Street Journal*, which put out
its first edition on July 8, 1889. As a most perceptive student of the stock market, he early reached
the conclusion that stocks do not go up and down
independently, but are affected, in a somewhat
magnetic way, by the rise and fall of business
conditions generally and by the current action of
many other stocks in the market. In other words,
he perceived that the up (bull) or down (bear)
trend in each stock is not an isolated performance but related to tidal trends in the market as
a whole.

From this line of reasoning the next steps were
quite obvious: (1) to select a small group of
representative stocks that might be followed
minutely day by day; (2) to average the performance of this group; and (3) to derive (and possibly project) from the variations in this average, rising or declining trends in the entire market, on the basis of which successful speculative
commitments might be made. Moreover, Dow
was convinced that these rising and falling markets would correspond quite faithfully to levels
of business activity as revealed in a representative index of industrial production. It is this part
of Dow's hypothesis that has fascinated so many
latter-day market speculators: (1) that stock
markets operate in up and down trends which

may actually predict and project their directions, often months ahead; and (2) that the stock market can act as an advance barometer of general business conditions. In acceptance of this theory, there is wide belief today that a significant decline in the stock market may foretell a decline in business activity, and in profits, a few months or a year later. Equally, strong bull markets on their way to new highs are thought to herald the tidings of good business for many months in the future.

THE DOW-JONES AVERAGES

To get the right combination of stocks for his average, Dow apparently tested out many individual issues and also varied the total number in the group designed to compose this average. For example, a twelve-stock average was used in his calculation between 1886 and 1896, and for part of that period (1889-96) a twenty-stock average was calculated as well. In 1897, his ideas about averages became more clarified, and he decided in that year that two averages should be used — one to check against the other — the Industrial and the Railroad averages, which are the indispensable ingredients of the Dow Theory today. Without attempting to list all the changes in the individual issues comprising these averages over the years, we are setting down below the component issues in the DJIA and DJRA in 1966.

THE 30 DOW-JONES INDUSTRIALS

Allied Chemical

Aluminum Co. of America

American Can

American Telephone &
Telegraph

American Tobacco

Anaconda

Bethlehem Steel

Chrysler

Du Pont

Eastman Kodak

General Electric

General Foods

General Motors

Goodyear

International Harvester

International Nickel

International Paper

Johns-Manville

Owens-Illinois

Procter & Gamble

Sears, Roebuck

Standard Oil (Calif.)

Standard Oil (N. J.)

Swift

Texaco

Union Carbide

United Aircraft

U. S. Steel

Westinghouse Electric

Woolworth

THE 20 DOW-JONES RAILS

Atchison, Topeka &
Santa Fe

Atlantic Coast Line

Canadian Pacific

Chesapeake & Ohio

Chicago & North Western

Delaware & Hudson

Denver & Rio Grande
Western

Great Northern

Illinois Central

Kansas City Southern

Louisville & Nashville

New York Central

Norfolk & Western

Pennsylvania

Seaboard Air Line

St. Louis-San Francisco

Southern Pacific

Southern Railway

Union Pacific

Western Pacific

Charles Dow, however, never developed anything like a complete theory or system that the
average trader today could use or follow in
making market decisions. The refinement of
Dow's theories of price movements and their relationship to business activity was the work of
two of his friends and followers. First, there was

S. A. Nelson, a reporter on *The Wall Street Journal*, who published, in 1902, *The ABC of Stock Speculation*. This book devoted several chapters to what he called "Dow's Theory." Following Nelson as Dow's friend and commentator was William Peter Hamilton, a reporter on *The Wall Street Journal* who became its editor in 1906 (Dow died in 1902). Hamilton wrote many feature articles about price movements, and in 1922 published his *Stock Market Barometer*, which for the first time attempted to establish a logical relationship between swings in the Dow-Jones averages and variations in levels of business activity. By devoting years to market studies and by constantly writing about them in *The Wall Street Journal*, Hamilton refined the Dow Theory to a degree that its originator would never have recognized. He developed what has proved to be a useful tool — almost a barometer — for businessmen, investors, and speculators to use in their projection and evaluation of trends in the stock market, and in business expansion and contraction.

Finally, as a student of the work of Dow, Nelson, and Hamilton, Robert Rhea has in recent years added some of the finishing touches to the Dow Theory and evolved certain rules and interpretations that have increased its practical usefulness to all those who thirst for guidance in divining future business and stock trends; and who hope to glean substantial profits, and even fortunes, by making the shrewd decisions at the right time.

THE DOW THEORY

Reduced to its simplest elements, the Dow Theory operates on the principle that the market tells its own story and prophesies its own future. By combining in one place (the stock exchange) the opinions, the estimates, and the judgments of all the people who buy and sell each day, the market is thought, in its own mystical way, to be foretelling the future. The ups and downs in the Dow-Jones averages do far more than indicate or reflect the earning power, dividend payments, and prospects of individual companies. They bear a barometric relationship to things to come. Accordingly, if your goal is to double your money by prudent and timely purchase of the right stocks, some knowledge and application of the Dow Theory may be not only useful but quite possibly rewarding.

HOW IT WORKS

The best practical exposition of this whole subject is Robert Rhea's *The Dow Theory*, written in 1932, and his subsequent book, *Dow Theory Revised*, which amplifies the first. If you want to become deeply indoctrinated in Dow, then read these works by Rhea. Meanwhile, you may get some useful market meat to chew on in the brief summary of this theory, and its applications, which follows.

The market is, like an ocean, always in motion. Movements are, according to the Dow Theory, threefold. There are first the day-to-day price movements, relatively narrow and not particularly revealing so far as any trend is concerned. The second movement is a middle-range one, often lasting for a month or two; and the third may last from three to five or more years — a full-scale bull or bear market, as the case may be. Obviously, the third movement creates the peaks or valleys, with the earlier part of this phase generating the most dramatic price swings.

Putting the theory in long-range perspective, the most important thing to determine is the primary long-term movement — the full-scale bull or bear market, which historically has ranged from two to six years.

The second element in the Dow Theory is what is called the secondary reaction. No bull market rises without interruption — a plateau or a setback — and no bear market declines without some intermediate rallies. Thus, these secondary reactions are important not only as brakes, or corrections, to major trends, but they are tricky and sometimes seem to indicate that a bull or bear market is at an end when, in truth, it is not. For example, the market break in May-June, 1962, eroded the DJIA by almost 30 percent, and some investors thought that this ended the bull market. Actually, the sell-off from 734.91 (a then all-time high) on December 12, 1961, and 146 in the Railroad average, to May 28 lows of 576.93 and 122.35, respectively, turned out to be merely a very energetic secondary reaction, an interlude in the bull market, which later soared, on February 9, 1966, to 995.15. The thing to note in this example of mid-1962 was the way in which the Rail average "confirmed" the action of the DJIA. Usually this confirming or "me, too" relationship of the Rail average is a somewhat lagging one. Most of the time the DJIA will lead the trendline, while the Rails tag along to confirm, or fail to deny, the correctness and validity of the direction indicated by the senior average.

Secondary reactions require skill for their detection. They generally last for three to four months and, on the average, will retrace about 50 percent of the price changes which have occurred since the end of the preceding secondary reaction. On charts, these reactions represent jagged lines which modify a long-range up- or downtrend.

The daily fluctuations in prices are given little value in Dow Theory. It's the primary trends and secondary reactions that tell the tale. And Dow attached great importance to the action of the Industrials and Rails in concert. A primary trend or a secondary reaction in DJIA is not official unless confirmed by the DJRA.

All of these market motions are revealed by charts which you'll find daily in *The Wall Street Journal,* and in a number of financial journals and investment-service letters. Many Dow fans like to keep their own charts, but this is not recommended unless you have a lot of time to devote to it, and are mathematically minded and meticulously accurate.

TOPS AND BOTTOMS

The most important markers in determining the primary trend are the making of new tops or bottoms in a current cycle. If, for example, the market reaches a new high and in its next decline stops at a point above the low points recorded in an earlier phase, then a bull market is indicated, and the chart may be expected in coming weeks to sawtooth to higher levels. Equally, if a previous low is penetrated, and the ensuing rally stops below the preceding high point, then a bear signal has been clearly given.

When the price movements of both DJIA and DJRA move in parallel and within a narrow price range (not more than 6 percent variation) for ten days or longer, this is called a line and its direction provides another classic Dow guideline. If this line points up, you may assume stocks are being accumulated (bullish). If the line is a downtrend, then you have evidence of distribution (bearish). There are some related theories, too, about volume: when volume dries up on rallies and increases on declines, a bear trend is indicated; and, conversely, when the market is listless on declines but in active volume on upturns, it's bullish. There is also a theory that all bull markets end with a roar — a selling climax with 12 to 14 million shares in daily volume.

The foregoing is obviously the sketchiest exposition of the Dow Theory. It was designed only as an outline; and if the theory really fascinates you, then read books on the subject, or seek out one of the market services that specialize in Dow technology.

HOW GOOD IS DOW?

There is a steady running argument among speculators about the validity and usefulness of the Dow Theory. On the record, it apparently called the end of the bear market in mid-1932, foretold the end of the bull market in 1937; and Hamilton blew the big whistle on the market in 1929. The rise in 1961 was outlined by a number of Dow charts. In August, 1962, a very clear call for a bull-market resumption was shown by Dow, and throughout 1964 the Dow signals were all bullish. A number of Dow followers believed that their charts defined the end of the bull market in May, 1966. As you may imagine, much of the market projection of Dow depends on individual interpretation of identical chart phenomena.

Many market operators have found the Dow Theory useful. Although by no means infallible, it is often used as a cross check on market decisions or opinions reached by other methods. Since a favorable market climate is so important to successful speculation in individual stocks, the Dow Theory should in no event be ignored.

DISTORTIONS

Perhaps the most common argument against the Dow Theory is that it is not equipped to evaluate properly, or in time, extraneous factors that affect the market: advances in government regulation and control over business, the forward moves of the welfare state, major defense decisions in Vietnam, price and wage controls, and the like. Further, such unpredictable action as changes in tax rates and the legal allowances for depreciation and obsolescence, and the change-over from war to peace production or vice versa, present uncertainties which the Dow method may not adequately take into account. Also, debt arrangements for acquisition of property alter trends in the economy. It makes a lot of difference in the construction industry whether a home buyer can make his purchase with 10 percent down or 40 percent down. In the motor industry, far more cars will be sold on thirty-six-month payments than on twenty-four. Even with all these variables to assimilate, however, the Dow Theory has apparently served with considerable barometric accuracy over the years, although it has been wrong on several occasions.

Many traders have complained that the Dow provides its signals too late. By the time the Dow bull or bear signals have been confirmed, they contend, a substantial part of the price swing has already occurred, reducing the profit potentials of commitments then made. Another criticism of Dow is that the Railroad average has lost its historic usefulness as a confirming factor, since transportation has moved so broadly into other areas — private cars, buses, airlines, pipelines, etc. Moreover, railroads are notably under intensive government regulation. Finally, critics say that thirty stocks are too few to project, or to represent, the action of the whole market; and that certain stocks with notable growth characteristics have quite disregarded the Dow trendline. Different issues in the DJIA would also have changed its course dramatically. If, for example, IBM had been included instead of AT&T, the DJIA today would be several hundred points higher!

Obviously this is no complete critique of Dow Theory. We would conclude that as a forecaster, it has served with considerable accuracy for over three generations; that while not perfect or infallible in appraisal of bull and bear swings over the years, it has been more often right than wrong; and that its major and most powerful signals given have, if acted upon, proved either protective or profitable. In any event, it is helpful in cross-checking or confirming market trends defined by other methods or techniques. Dow is a useful tool and may, on occasion, help you double your market money.

6

the right climate for successful stock speculation

It is obvious that the stock or stocks you buy are more likely to go up if the whole market is rising. Thus, in soaring bull markets, the gainers may outnumber the losers, day after day, at a 2 to 1 to 4 to 1 ratio. In such markets it is not particularly difficult to make money, with the odds averaging roughly 3 to 1 in your favor. Equally, however, markets of such delightful buoyancy may be nearing, or at, a top, so that nimble trading footwork may be required if you are to cash in before a downtrend causes your profits to vanish like butter in the noonday sun.

Thus, fundamental to your success in stocks is a proper awareness as to whether you are in a bull market and, if so, how far along in it. If the market has entered or verged on a period of declining prices (a bear market), then you should probably (1) consider selling certain stocks, (2) defer purchases you had in mind, or (3) have especially compelling reasons for buying a particular stock.

To provide valuable guidance as to whether or not the market climate is such as to encourage and reward speculation for the rise, a look at past performances may be helpful. In the past fifty-five years, it is possible to observe that stocks have gone through many major price cycles — commonly called bull and bear markets — all of which have required a considerable time for their completion. These cycles, moreover, appear to be influenced greatly by, and often to precede by a few months, rising and falling tides in the profitability and general activity of business. The early phases of these bull markets were obviously ideal times for buying; and the early phases of bear markets ideal for selling.

UNPREDICTABLE SWINGS

Nice as this theory of majestic and systematic ebb and flow of share prices and business activity is, in practice the height, depth, and duration of these swings have proved most erratic and quite unpredictable. This is true because there have always been so many variable factors: war, cold war, or peace; capital investment, interest rates; wage rates, levels of debt; technological advances; productivity of labor; expenditures for welfare; and the economic philosophies of the political parties in power. Historically, stocks in certain industries have been especially sensitive and responsive (up as well as down) to cyclical conditions. Such equities as copper, steel, railroad, textile, and machine-tool shares have traditionally been classified as cyclical issues and characterized by wide price swings. Among defense issues such as utilities, and food and tobacco companies (wherein demand for goods or services tends to continue even during business recession), cyclical swings also occur, but usually within narrower price ranges; while growth stocks tend to be less depressed in bear markets and to rise to new heights at the top of bull markets.

Just for background, there follows a tabulation of market swings running back for several years. You will observe that the longest bull market lasted, with minor setbacks, from 1949 to 1962; and many regard the 30 percent decline of the latter year as but a correction in a bull market still in robust health as this was written, January 11, 1967.

MARKET MILESTONES

		DJIA
8/8/45	Russia declares war on Japan	161.83
8/14/45	Japan surrenders	164.79
6/3/46	Italy votes 6 to 5 for republic	211.47
11/24/46	Communists register 2½ million out of 8 million in French election	165.10
12/30/49	Average crosses 200 for first time since 8/21/46	200.52
5/23/50	General Motors concludes 5-year labor contract with 4¢ an hour annual escalation	222.47
3/22/54	Following, by 5 days, cut of rediscount rate from 3¼% to 3% on 3/17/54, market crosses 300	301.60
1/3/55	General Motors proposes $325 million expansion, and market tops 400	408.89
3/12/56	Mollet becomes French Premier and Dow crosses 500	500.24
7/25/57	Republic of Tunisia established —highest postwar Dow high	516.69
12/18/57	Indonesia nationalizes Dutch businesses, and market hits cyclical low	426.18
1/4/60	Steel companies settle 120-day strike	679.06
10/25/60	Cuba has confiscated $1.5 billion in American property	566.05

		DJIA
5/17/61	Dow reaches new high above 700	705.52
12/31/61	New DJIA record high	734.91
6/26/62	Dow-Jones 4-year low	536.27
11/6/62	Buoyant recrossing of the 600 mark	610.48
9/15/63	New Malaysian Federation and new market high	740.13
11/22/63	President Kennedy assassinated	711.49
2/26/64	$11.5 billion income tax reduction	799.38
2/9/66	All-time DJIA high	995.15
10/7/66	Correction to yearly low	744.32
1/11/67	Market after President's State of Union speech	822.49

THE ROAR OF INFLATION NEXT?

In the longer panoramic sweep, you might say that 1929 marked the end of the New Era (Dow high, 381) and the gateway to the Great Depression; 1932, the depths, with the Dow Average bottoming at 41. In 1946, came the postwar boom and removal of price controls (Dow, 211.47); the era of rising abundance came in 1956, with the Dow crossing 500; then, in 1959, the temporary inflation crest (topping at the 1/4/60 level of 679.06). Finally, we saw the new-issue splurge of 1961, with the Dow reaching 734.91; and the exalted Great Society peak (995.15), February, 1966. Our question now is: Is this the

regional high, or is the 1,000 zone almost penetrated in 1966 a prelude and a launching pad for
new uncharted altitudes based on an inflation
out of hand? We have great propellants for inflation: (1) an inexorable increase in the cost of
government; (2) an inexorable increase in the
price of labor; (3) an inexorable increase in
the level of debt — government, corporate, realty
mortgage, and personal; and (4) a steady expansion in the money supply.

A look back at these big bull-market top-outs
reveals no formula or basis for determining in
the future how high the present bull market will
go, or how long it will last. As a rough general-
ization, the market, in receding from an historic high point, may descend 30 percent or more
from that high within eighteen to twenty-four
months, and the level then reached may be regarded as reasonably favorable for bullish operation. (But no two swings are ever identical.)

Many informed economists and financial
authorities think that we have done much to
flatten out, and possibly to prevent, recessions
or depressions in the future. Those who argue
this point to all the "floors" now in place under
our economy: minimum-wage laws, unemployment insurance, guaranty of deposits in banks
and savings-and-loan associations; credit insurance covering personal loans; amortized
long-term home mortgages; Social Security
and huge pension and retirement funds, stabilizing and assuring income for the senior population; Medicare and hospitalization insurance;

steadily rising levels of personal income, savings, and investment; and sustained high levels of government expenditure.

If all this is true, and if indeed we have tamed the business cycle, then our prospects for successful short-run speculation appear most promising. Almost any time will be a hopeful time for aggressive speculation on this premise. In any event, February 9, 1966, marked a Dow-Jones high of 995.15, and the crest of a five-year surge to the most impressive business and stock-market highs in history.

Everyone thought the DJIA would cross 1,000 in 1966, but 995.18 proved the top closing price not only for the year but, so far, for all time. A zig-zag downtrend led the way to a yearly low of 744.32 on October 7, 1966, accounted for, in considerable measure, by substantial liquidations in many issues by institutional investors. Many professionals felt that the bull market was really at an end. In any event, the share volume of trading on the New York Stock Exchange attributed to institutions and their intermediaries was reported to be 32.3 percent of the total on October 19, 1966—an all-time high.

But institutional and individual bears were wrong. Considerable market buoyancy developed before the year end, and 1967 opened with a bang. The market advanced for twenty-one days out of the first twenty-five in January, neared 850 on DJIA, and set the stage for measured market optimism in 1967. Many market professionals who had sold in October returned to the "buy" side encouraged by lower interest rates and 1966 earnings reports, many at historic highs. Further, the President's decision to press only for a 6 percent surtax was bullish, as many had expected a heavier tax bite.

Before taking for granted the maintenance of these giddy levels and continuously confident markets as a sort of ever-normal granary, however, we should observe certain assorted phenomena that should accompany and support a high level of economic activity and general enthusiasm for stocks.

In general, the economy appears unlikely to decline seriously when (1) the price/earnings multiple of the DJIA is no higher than 17; (2) interest rates are steady or rising moderately; (3) Gross National Product is increasing annually at the rate of 3 percent or more; (4) annual capital investment by corporations is steady or rising; (5) income-tax rates are unchanged or being reduced; (6) housing starts are equal to or ahead of last year; (7) stock margin requirements are stabilized or unlikely to be increased; (8) time spans for repayment of installment debt are not being shortened; (9) national savings are 6 percent or more of disposable income; and (10) unemployment does not exceed 5 percent.

Of course, if, despite all these sturdy bulwarks and safeguards, a recession does emerge and we enter a market climate hostile to rising prices, then we should be prepared to do two things: (1) sell out weaker and more volatile holdings and those in declining earnings trends; or (2) sell short. This latter tactic, while highly functional in declining markets, seems to go against the grain of most Americans. The idea of selling a stock not owned today and buying it back 10, 15, or 20 points lower, weeks or months later, violates our national trait of unquenchable optimism. Further, the relatively few market traders who do sell short are an "itchy" lot; and most lack the requisite patience or nerve. They "buy back" to cover their short positions too soon. For the average avid trader, we do not recommend short selling, even though at certain times it might prove most profitable. We would prefer to recommend selling selected holdings outright; and/or awaiting more propitious market conditions, before purchasing properly researched shares designed to generate rewarding gains. In any event, the more uncertain market conditions are, the better and stronger should be the stocks selected for your purchase or retention. In weak markets, less entrenched and unseasoned equities are most vulnerable, and earlier high fliers often fall fastest and farthest. In wobbly markets, nothing recedes like excess!

7

market brakes and boosters

Operating quite independently of positive or negative trends in individual companies and industries are the vital decisions made by the monetary authorities. Easy credit and low interest rates have, as we observed earlier, provided a powerful upthrust in the early phases of bull markets; and at all stages the price and availability of credit have a pervasive and, on occasion, a dominant influence on stock prices. Moreover, the ends of bull markets have consistently occurred when the credit structure became top-heavy and wobbly. Markets stop going up when buyers run out of money—i.e., have extended their credit to the full.

Accordingly, in making successful market decisions and in so timing speculative sorties that they produce profits, a hard and continuous look at monetary conditions is essential. The changing terms on which money is available actually operate as either brakes or boosters to stock prices. Operation of the money mechanism is increasingly a function of the welfare state and the Great Society, in an endeavor to exert directional and dimensional control over the economy—in peace, war, and between elections!

MONETARY CONTROLS

There are three major controls over the money supply that are important to investors: (1) stock-market margin requirements; (2) the Federal Reserve Bank rediscount rate; and (3) the size of the reserves that member banks must maintain in Federal Reserve banks. While the third control is, of course, important, it is much less publicized, and we can derive adequate guidance for speculative operations by watching the first two—stock margins and the rediscount rate. As and when these are increased, they exert a braking and restraining influence on stock prices. If they are low or lowered, they are definitely market boosters.

Since the end of World War II, the monetary authorities have used the mechanisms of easing and tightening money like a Yo-Yo. In the twenty years ending June 1, 1966, we have had 128 months of relatively easy money and 116 months of tightening credit. Since the creation of the Federal Reserve System, in 1913, the New York rediscount rate has been increased thirty-six times and reduced forty times. The relationship of these undulations in money supply to swings in the stock market is illustrated in the accompanying ten-year chart.

There are several important observations to be drawn. Generally speaking, the longer the period of easy-money conditions, the longer will be the ensuing period of rising stock prices. However, one increase in the rediscount rate or one increase in the margin rate is seldom serious enough to disturb or slow down an upswing in stocks very much; but if there is a series of rises, the warning signals of a cresting stock market begin to fly.

For example, on March 6, 1959, the rediscount rate was advanced from 3 to 3.5 percent; then to 4 percent before the end of the year. During 1960, the rediscount rate was reduced from 4 to 3.5 percent and then from 3.5 to 3 percent. This ushered in an easy-money period and an upsurge in stock prices that continued (with only a 30 percent setback in 1962) until February, 1966.

After 1960, you will note the next change in the discount rate was an increase in the summer of 1963. The money savants in Washington felt

TEN-YEAR CHART SHOWING DOW-JONES INDUSTRIALS, MARGIN REQUIREMENTS, AND REDISCOUNT RATE

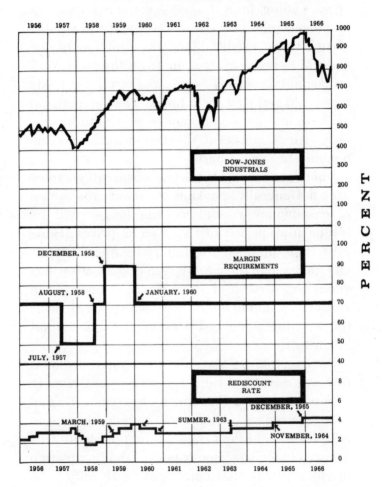

that the boom was advancing too rapidly, so the rediscount rate was raised to 3.5 percent. Then, when President Johnson was elected, in November, 1964, the rediscount rate was raised again — this time to 4 percent. Finally, on December 6, 1965, the rate was pushed up again — this time without the blessing of the President — to 4.5 percent. Within the next two months, the market reached an all-time high of 995.15. Thus, after three rises in the discount rate, there was evidence that investors were running out of money, and at least this phase of the bull market appeared at an end. On the record, one of the best ways to restore exuberant confidence in the stock market would be a reduction in the rediscount rate, triggering the start of another credit cycle. Just as a raise in interest rates dampens market enthusiasm, a lowering kindles it.

MARGIN REQUIREMENTS

Even more directly related to those who trade or invest in stocks is the margin rate — the maximum percentage of loans to market valuation of listed stocks available to investors when they borrow to buy securities from a brokerage house. Obviously, this loan ratio creates a significant leverage. When margins are low, investors can acquire a lot more stock (per dollar of their own money); and buying power thus generated heats up the market.

Referring again to the chart, you will see that

margins were reduced to 50 percent in mid-1957, and that the market reacted so swiftly to this happy event that the requirements were upped to 70 percent in August, 1958; and then to 90 percent before the year was out. These actions, tied in closely with the rise in the discount rate in 1958, caused the market to top out in 1959. It did not start to turn up again until, within a single month in 1960, first the rediscount rate was lowered to 3.5 percent, and then the margin ratio lowered to 70 percent (and maintained there since). There is thus great significance in these money changes, especially when both interest and margin rates are adjusted within a short time of each other. The speculative climate can be reversed almost overnight just by pulling these money levers; and the market may dramatically change both its character and its direction, disregarding for the moment major trends in corporate earnings or dividends.

What can we summarize from these oscillatory monetary decisions? What useful guidance do these accordion-like expansions and contractions in money and credit offer to nimble speculators? There appear to be five major derivative axioms: (1) monetary changes are among the earliest and most dependable indicators of market turning points; (2) rediscount reductions move markets up, more and faster than increases dampen them; (3) reaction to discount changes may take from three to six months; (4) a series of changes — preferably three — in either direction, in the rediscount rate, can exert a predictable future influence on speculative enthusiasm and on stock prices; and (5) margin changes have a more immediate but a less lasting effect on market action (probably because margin regulations affect far fewer people — i.e., only those who borrow from brokers to buy).

Between the two, adjusting the rediscount rate (either up or down) makes a far heavier and more lasting impact on share prices than do changes in margin requirements. Interest rates might be regarded as the planets, and margins as the satellites. When the prevailing rediscount rate is 4.5 percent (or higher) and when margin requirements are 90 percent or more, you will buy few cheap stocks. Don't fight the brakes — wait for the boosters.

From the foregoing, and especially from the chart, you can see how important it is, if you are to make — or double — your money in the market, that you relate your commitments to the cost and availability of money, and to swift and frequently unheralded changes in these economic markets. Money can be a market brake or booster. Decide which it is likely to be before you buy!

8

growth stocks for
rapid gains

In the past decade, "growth stocks" have fascinated Wall Street, and investors were well
on their way to rich market rewards if they
owned and held such dazzling performers as
IBM, Xerox, Syntex, Cenco Instruments, Mc-
Graw-Hill, Franklin Life, etc. Such authentic
growth issues not only have rewarded patient
long-term holders well, but have also turned in
outstanding performances within a single year.
For example, Fairchild Camera in 1965 rose from

27 1/2 to 150 1/2 — a gain of 447.3 percent!

Further, an examination of the annual performance of outstanding stocks in the past six years reveals that an important percentage of them were growth stocks. Accordingly, in our unremitting search for stocks that can double within a year, it's important to be able to recognize a growth stock, to distinguish it from its less animate brethren, and to select from the group individual issues of unusual near-term promise.

CHARACTERISTICS OF GROWTH STOCKS

As a general rule, growth stocks are found in growing industries. In 1965 the "hot" industries were airlines and TV companies; and twelve doublers, growth stocks all, scored in these two stellar groups. Growth industries are pretty obvious: electronics, aircraft and space-age companies, business machines, publishing, hospital supply, apparel, beverages, food products, water treatment, service companies, motels, space-age metals, etc. These industries are all growing far faster than the Gross National Product. They fill rising demands generated by the population explosion and the constant and substantial uptrend in per capita incomes throughout the free world.

It does not follow, however, that all common stocks of companies located in growth industries are automatically growth stocks. Far from it. There are stragglers, marginal members, inefficient units, and nonsurvivors even in the most rapidly expanding economic sectors. Consider, for example, that over eight hundred motorcar companies have been formed since 1900. These all started out in one of the most amazing growth industries the world has ever known. Yet how many of their stocks proved to be growth stocks? Most fell by the wayside, and there are only four significant American motorcar companies today. As a growth stock, General Motors has been a dazzler; but whatever became of Moon, Marmon, Jackson, Velie, Dort, Dobie, and Franklin? Thus, random selection of stocks, just because they are equities in a burgeoning industry, is not enough. A growth company must document, first, its capacity to survive and, second, its ability to earn and expand profits at an inordinate rate.

Equally, not all growth stocks are found in growing industries. In the coal industry, for instance, there has been a long-range decline since 1925, yet some splendidly growing companies and historic market performers have emerged in this fading economic sector — Peabody Coal and Joy Manufacturing (coal machinery), for example.

BENCH MARKS

One good way to screen and select growth stocks is to seek the best managed and most profitable companies in zooming industries. These may not be the largest units in their group, and, for our purposes, smaller companies in an early corporate phase are often the most dramatic gainers. It is, for example, much easier for a company to double its sales from $10 million annually to $20 million than for a larger company to go from $100 million to $200 million in sales. Small and middle-sized companies usually grow fastest. These are more difficult to pick out since they are less well known, appear on few investment or brokerage house "recommended" lists, and their shares often trade inactively in the over-the-counter market. Growth is always most dynamic in its earlier phases. A child grows much faster between one and ten than between ten and twenty!

With the above background guidelines in mind, we are now ready to list the particular qualities or characteristics we should seek in growth stocks that may lead to swift market gains within a single year.

CRITERIA FOR SELECTION OF GROWTH STOCKS

1. A growth stock should have doubled its sales in the past five years; or show a sales expansion at the rate of at least 12 percent annually compounded.

2. Net earnings should be increasing at a rate of at least 12 percent a year compounded; and in well-managed companies, net should rise at a faster rate than sales.

3. The subject industry should be growing at

least twice as fast as the economy as a whole.

4. Growth should be not only rapid but consistent. An erratic company that increases its net earnings 70 percent in one year and five percent the next would not qualify. Investors and market traders are partial to growth stocks, à la IBM, where substantial gains in net have been recorded *without interruption* year after year.

5. Management should be aggressive, imaginative, research-minded, cost-conscious, and energetic. In early-phase companies, dynamic management is often supplied by ambitious younger men trained and successful in big companies but seeking larger rewards and greater personal freedom as part owners and directors of their own companies. Good management is often the lengthened shadow of a single outstanding individual: "Tex" Thornton at Litton Industries, the late Thomas Watson at IBM, Alfred Sloan at General Motors, Dr. Emery Land at Polaroid, Charles Becker at Franklin Life, Dr. Armand Hammer at Occidental Petroleum, Leon Hess at Hess Oil, General Sarnoff at RCA, for example. Betting on an authentic business or technical genius can be one of the most rewarding techniques for long-range or shorter-term market success.

6. The management group should be made up of large stockholders. If a substantial amount of stock (usually 30 percent or more) is held by management men, then they are likely to seek the same thing you do — rising wealth through

capital gains. A hungry, stock-minded management is a common characteristic of a growth
company.

7. Plowback is important. Growth companies
in general go in heavily for retained earnings,
and the fastest growing ones seldom pay out
more than 35 percent of net in cash in any year.
Of all the companies whose stocks have doubled
in a single year, very few will be found that
pay out over 50 percent of net in cash. (Life-
insurance stocks, which scored notable market
advances between 1954 and 1964, seldom pay
out in cash more than 15 percent of net.)

This conserving of cash and reinvestment of
profits is in fact a most important ingredient
in growth companies. Retention of funds makes
it less necessary to seek new outside capital
for expansion (which also may dilute stockholders' equity); and it is also preferred by high-
bracket stockholders, who would rather have
their income from market gains, taxable at only
25 percent, than from cash dividends, taxable
at 50 percent or higher. Heavy annual plowback builds up book value and enhances future
earning power; and both of these corporate
gains promote higher market evaluations of the
subject common stocks.

8. In a well-managed growth company, profit
margins (conversion of gross into net) are consistently high; and there is usually a tendency
for profit margins to widen. In fact, even though
sales are rising, if profit margins have declined

noticeably for two or more years in a row, you're probably in the wrong growth stock!

9. A good growth company is steadily driving to make money. Therefore, it should show a consistently high return on stockholders' equity (the book value of its common stock). As a general rule, a growth company should earn not less than 15 percent on stockholders' equity annually. This percentage might dip in a particular year due to some unusual corporate expenditure for new facilities, or to costly research of a new product; but as a rule "performance" stocks will earn 15 percent to 25 percent on stock equity with considerable regularity.

10. Growth stocks, to generate market gains, must be bought prudently. It's perfectly possible to pay too much even for the best growth stock. A friend of mine lost $80,000 in 1962 buying IBM at 555 and seeing it melt miserably in the erosive June market sun of that year. In general, growth stocks should be bought before they have become widely acclaimed in the market, and preferably at a price/earnings multiple of no more than 15. Market prices of 60 and 70 times earnings are almost always overvaluations; and they are discounting the growth factor too far into the future. Most growth-stock buyers, whether they purchase for a trading swing (our approach) or long-term gain, develop some notions about future market potentials. A practical way to project hoped-for gains is merely to add the growth rate of the latest per-share

net earnings of a company for the next four years and multiply the results by the *average* price/earnings multiple of the stock for the preceding four years.

To illustrate, suppose a growth stock, Glitter Electronics, earned $1 in 1966, with an indicated annual growth rate of 20 percent. Then, for 1967, the net figure would be $1.20; in 1968, $1.44; in 1969, $1.73; and in 1970, $2.08. Assuming an average multiple of 20, then Glitter Electronics common selling at 20 in 1966 might be worth 24 in 1967; rise to 28 7/8 in 1968; 35 1/2 in 1969; and 41 1/2 in 1970. This rough calculation may understate the ultimate market action in the stock, because (1) the figuring is straight arithmetic without compounding the earnings annually; (2) growth may be at a faster rate; (3) the company may achieve a technological breakthrough that will "romance" the issue and may excite speculators' fancies so that the stock becomes glamorous, like Solitron or Valley Metallurgical, and sell at multiples of 30 or more; (4) the stock may be sought for acquisition by a larger and better known company; and (5) a heavy demand for the stock, with only a small floating supply, may rocket the price of the issue due to its scarcity.

Obviously, in the stocks we seek, some special stimulation must take place, since a price rise of 20 percent in 1967 (from 20 to 24) falls far short of our profit expectations. Even in growth stocks we should always be looking for some plus factor that may make the issue perform not just well, but sensationally. The particular stock we look for should resemble Kentucky Fried Chicken, which, on remarkable earnings, rose from an original subscription price of $15 (in April, 1966) to well past $30 in less than six months. Villager, Inc., a dynamic apparel company, also doubled within a year. Growth stocks on today's shopping list might include Chicago Musical Instruments, a Canadian oil such as Canadian Superior, Occidental Petroleum, Florida Gas, Kaiser Industries, Iowa Beef Packers, Ocean Drilling & Exploration. This is no official list of growth-type companies (we have a screened list of 40 diversified selections for possible 100 percent gain later on in the book). These companies were cited merely because they illustrate the kinds of growth record, or potentials for growth, that in the past have generated unusual stock profits.

In all this discussion about growth stocks, however, it must be observed that there is nothing inevitable about growth. A company can expand remarkably for a few years and then either stop growing or go into a tailspin. The bowling industry, and such leaders therein as Brunswick and American Machine & Foundry, illustrate this. In 1959-60, it appeared that America was going to do nothing in its spare time but bowl, and these two companies surged ahead in the market, turning out bowling equipment and helping to finance hundreds of new bowling emporia, complete with automatic pin-spotters, restaurant facilities, and the rest of the works. When the bowling mania subsided, stocks in what had seemed a dazzling growth industry cooled off, and American Machine and Brunswick stockholders saw market profits in these issues vanish like snow upon the desert's dusty wastes.

CONCLUSION

We conclude as we started, with solid endorsement of growth stocks for market gain. We have set down some sensible criteria for selection of growth issues that should be helpful in screening possible winners. Equally, we have pointed out that growth is not necessarily a "forever" thing. Growth rates, both in industries and in individual companies, can change, slow down, or reverse.

In market performance, the leading New York Stock Exchange growing industrial groups in 1966 were: air transport, up 14 percent; cosmetics, up 13 percent; electronics, up 25.5 percent; motion pictures, up 23 percent; radio and TV broadcasting, up 30.5 percent; and sulphur, up 19 percent. The "turkeys" were: trucking, down 27.5 percent; cigars, down 50 percent; textile products, down 36 percent; steel, off 38 percent; savings-and-loan holding companies, off 25 percent; chemicals, off 31 percent; shipbuilding, off 35 percent; and cement, off 30 percent. For 1967, the likeliest industrial groups for gain may include the depressed ones of 1966 — S&L stocks, life-insurance stocks, and trucking companies; and ascending ones, such as offshore drillers, airlines, computer manufacturers, publishers, plastics, ocean research, electronics, instrumentation, medical and hospital supplies, and possibly a resurgence in the building-materials group.

In growth stocks, as in all others, there are the imponderable factors — the whims and caprices of speculators, the changing fashions of the market, and the unpredictable valuations a mass of speculators will place on earnings in different companies — 55 times earnings for Xerox, when General Motors sells at 10 times, Florida Power & Light at 26, and Comsat, with no record of earnings, sells at $42 a share. Obviously, speculation is far more of an art than a science, and if we hope to double our money in a single year, luck may be far more important than profound knowledge and wisdom of the marketplace!

9

special situations and cyclical stocks

Another likely area for creation of unusual market gains is found among "special situations." A special situation is not just a stock that brokerage houses or investment services are boldly recommending. It is a corporate security that may advance rapidly due to internal factors within the company itself and usually not related to market conditions or trends generally. Also, a special situation will often provide above-average downside protection, due to the solidity of its book value, or its record of stability in earnings and dividends. The market "romance," however, will stem from some unusual development.

Most commonly, a special situation is created by prospects of merger or acquisition, sale or liquidation of corporate assets, a corporate reorganization or reclassification. The important thing to look for in each special situation is the plus factor or unique feature that may cause the stock to be worth a lot more money in a relatively short period of time.

MERGERS

As mergers are the commonest special propellants, we'll look at them first. In almost every case, the smaller company (the one being bought out) will prove the more attractive and rewarding speculation. For example, the stock of McWood Corporation, listed on the American Stock Exchange, was trading at around $10 a share in early December of 1966. McWood had established quite a growth record, increasing its net by 400 percent in the years 1962-66. McWood built up a system of regional pipelines for gathering crude oil, principally from individual oil producers, and selling and delivering it to oil buyers miles away from the wellheads. The company earnings had flattened out in 1965 and 1966 to around $1.30 a share; and the stock had rather languished in market interest. Perceptive investors, however, might have foreseen in Mc-

Wood Corporation a stock potentially attractive as an acquisition for a larger oil company; but the apparent plateau of earnings and absence of dividends cast no dramatic aura over the stock in the fall of 1966. Suddenly, however, McWood "caught on," and in the first three weeks of December, the issue rose swiftly from 10 to 16. On December 15, the cause became apparent, with the press announcement that Occidental Petroleum (a dynamic growth company) had offered to acquire McWood on the basis of .4 share of Occidental common for each share of McWood. With Occidental selling then at around 40, the indicated value of McWood became 16.

McWood common, when it sold at $10 a share, was a good example of a potential special situation. At 16, the possibilities for gain were by no means at an end, because (1) Occidental Petroleum itself was a stock in a strong upward trend; (2) if the proposal of acquisition was not approved, somebody else might make an even better bid for McWood; and (3) if McWood stockholders did not, in sufficient number, vote to accept the exchange offer, perhaps Occidental might move aggressively to buy McWood common in the open market, possibly at still higher prices. McWood at 10 had a prospect of doubling (or nearly so) its market price within a year. It actually gained 60 percent in three weeks. Occidental, meanwhile, advanced a little, but nothing like 60 percent.

Other stocks that qualified as special situations (merger-type) in 1966 were Random House, which advanced briskly prior to merger into Radio Corporation; Standard & Poor's, which merged with McGraw-Hill; and, in 1965, Jefferson Lake Petrochemicals, which rose well over 100 percent as stock control moved into the hands of Occidental Petroleum.

Quite frequently, however, contemplated mergers fail to jell. In 1966, Cities Service made offers for both United Nuclear and Hugoton Production. Neither acquisition proposal was ratified, however, and, as this was written (Jan. 11, 1967), Hugoton, which had sold as high as 58, was selling at 40. It does not appear over-priced at that quotation, either as an independent natural-gas producer or as future merger-bait for some other eager company. Prentice-Hall was widely rumored as a merger candidate at around 40, and the stock traded up to 65 (Jan. 11, 1967), even though no merger materialized.

Mergers are being brainstormed every business day in Wall Street houses. In 1966, a record number of corporate consolidations — 2,377 — took place, with about 60 percent all-cash transactions and the balance employing equity and debt securities. The favorite merger wampum (after cash) in 1966 was the convertible preferred, and in that year forty-four new issues of that description were listed on NYSE (against fifteen in 1965). This class of security offers the advantages of a tax-free vehicle in an exchange offer and a senior (and more recession-resistant) security with a highly dependable dividend, and usually provides a better investment yield than the common exchanged for it. These convertible preferreds are especially attractive in a slack or declining stock market, as they protect quite well against market erosion yet provide an opportunity for substantial gain if the market surges upward.

A FEW EXAMPLES

Radio Corporation offered a $4 convertible preferred to shareholders of Hertz Corporation; Diamond Alkali offered a $2 convertible (each into 1.15 shares of common) to stockholders of Nopco Chemical; Teledyne offered one share of $3.50 convertible preferred for each three shares of Vasco common held; U. S. Plywood offered 4/10 share of common plus one share of a new $1.20 convertible preferred for each acquired share of Champion Paper. These and similar convertible preferred or preference shares themselves qualify as special situations.

Almost invariably the stock of the smaller company, being swallowed up in acquisition, will develop a swift price run-up; but doubling your money in such a situation in a single year is rather unusual. Rapid rises of 10 percent to 40 percent are not uncommon, but you have to be prescient, or just plain lucky, to get a twelve-month doubler via the merger route. The odds are mathematically more favorable, however, if the stock being acquired sells below 20 before the fireworks start.

MERGER-MINDED COMPANIES

Companies that make a career of arranging mergers might qualify as special situations. For example, Greatamerica assembled 17 percent of Franklin Life stock (which it sold to Continental Insurance in 1966); and later acquired 80 percent of Braniff Airlines, which shortly began to flower. A company with the resources and management of Greatamerica can develop impressive gains in asset value by its skill and strategic timing in entry into or exit from strategically selected major investment positions.

Walter Kidde & Company common, listed on NYSE, swung in 1966 between 36 and 74 1/4, animated by its skill in consummating productive mergers. Litton grew great by the merger route and makes regular headlines in Wall Street with its acquisitions — proposed, considered, or consummated. Gulf & Western Industries, Textron, Glen Alden, and the like are perennial special situations by virtue of their zeal for mergers.

To get a stock that can double from a merger development, scan the financial pages carefully and regularly; and concentrate on the likeliest industries for merging — publishing, trucking, small electronic or instrument or scientific companies, realty companies, retailers, insurance, liquefied petroleum gas (LPG) and independent telephone companies. In a good market climate, a small company with an exciting future can become merger-bait and generate swift and sizable market profits. Be on the lookout for such opportunities, and act boldly when you've found a superior one!

SPIN-OFFS

Another special situation with a fine history of profitability is the spin-off. Here a sizable company, for some reason — corporate policy, antitrust action, monopoly charges, desiring to discontinue a certain line of production or subordinate operations, or whatever it may be — may deliver to its stockholders certain assets, proceeds from sale thereof, or actual shares of a hitherto affiliated property or company. Almost always this spin-off is profitable to prior holders of the mother-company shares; and frequently the spin-off shares may enhance in market value rapidly.

There are a lot of good examples. In 1958, Ogden Corporation spun off Syntex stock by permitting its stockholders to buy one share of Syntex at $2 for each four shares of Ogden owned. This Syntex stock sold as high as 124 3/4 in 1966, equivalent (after a 3-for-1, and then a 2-for-1 split) to $748.50 for each original $2 share!

Alico Land Development Company shares were given, in 1960, to Atlantic Coast Line Company stockholders (one share of Alico for each share of Coast Line). Alico common was immediately worth $8.50 a share. Hilton International Corporation was spun off to Hilton Hotels Corporation stockholders in 1964 — one share of

International for each two of Hilton Hotels owned. The tail has actually wagged the dog, and Hilton International, operator of a global chain of glamorous hotels, has become the "inn" stock of the jet set, sold at 35 in December, 1966, and was then being romanced for possible acquisition for TWA.

You learn about spin-offs from reading financial pages and journals. Note when a company must divest certain properties by court order, or plans to get out of a sector of its business. Do some sleuthing to learn the possible value of the existing assets. It's often better (and takes less money) to buy the new spun-off stock than to buy the old company shares and await the corporate molting. The biggest spin of 1966-67 was the exit from Grinnell Corporation (sprinklers) of American District Telegraph, Holmes Electric Protective Company, and Automatic Fire Alarm Company. The Supreme Court had earlier ruled that ownership by Grinnell of all these created a corporate monopoly in burglar and fire-alarm protection.

MISCELLANEOUS SPECIAL SITUATIONS

Certain special situations exist when a company established in one line of business enters, or develops a position in, another and perhaps more romantic field. Storer Broadcasting bought heavily into Northeast Airlines at $4 a share just as air-transport stock began to zoom in 1965; and Storer common attracted as a result a strong market following. Freeport Sulphur doubled in a few weeks, not from its sulphur business but from an exciting copper strike on extensive acreage in Timmins, Ontario.

Other special situations would include tenders —offers to buy either by an outside company or by a company seeking to purchase its own stock. Tender offers are usually made at above the existing market price for an issue, and customarily for a specific number of shares. On occasion, if the tender offer does not bring in enough stock, the price may be increased or the company making the offer may decide to buy heavily in the open market. Seldom do tenders set the stage for a short-term 100 percent gain, but moderate gains from this source are not only possible but reasonably predictable.

Reorganization offers opportunities for the bold because the launching of a new capitalization by scaling down debts of the old one ushers in new hope and confidence—essential elements in making any stock go up. A tired company named Avien, Inc., went into Chapter XI Bankruptcy (which does not require sale of assets to satisfy creditors) in 1964, and its common sold in pennies. Then, after the company was able to lift itself from Chapter XI, the stock rose to 4 1/4 in 1966. Fortunes were made in the railway reorganizations of the late 1930's.

Still other special situations are found in companies with interesting patent potentials: Permeator Corporation, with a special method for improving oil recovery; Multi-Minerals, Ltd., with a patented way to process low-grade potash ores; Millipore Corporation, with a patent making possible the canning of draft beer; and Tool Research and Development, with a patent on a honeycomb-welded steel useful in jet and space-craft. Shares in such companies often assay high in romance and low in near-term earnings. Comsat (Communications Satellite) may one day sell at $200, but the earnings to justify such a gaudy evaluation are not yet in view.

From the above, you can see that special situations come by the dozen. No two are alike, and all depend on something more than a fundamental projection of indicated future earnings or dividends. Special situations are the "biological sports" of speculation.

CYCLICAL STOCKS

Stocks in this category may resemble special situations, but their dynamics for gain depend more on timing than on any other factor. While, over a period of years, most of the companies with annual sales of over $200 million will steadily increase in earnings, there are certain ones whose profit progress is jagged and uneven. They make a lot of money in boom years, but their earnings may drop off rapidly in slack or depressed times. Companies with these characteristics are called cyclical, and their stocks, purchased at the right times, may provide excellent opportunities for doubling one's money.

The building-and-construction industry is a typically cyclical one. When housing, office-building, new plant construction, and road-building are going full blast (as in 1963-64), steel, cement, lumber, gypsum, mortgage, and plumbing companies will reap peak profits, and their stock will command high market prices as a result.

When building slackens, however, as it did in 1965-66, then stocks in this sector fade. Good examples are cement, steel, and savings-and-loan shares in this period. They sold in 1966 as much as 50 percent below their 1962-64 highs. Railroads and machine tools are usually included in the cyclical group. In a later chapter, which lists stocks that doubled in 1965, you'll see this cyclical group appropriately represented.

In conclusion, cyclical stocks can be a lush field for sensational market gains, but they must be bought when business is rising from a setback and not at an historic high. It appears possible that 1967 may present some golden opportunities among the cyclicals. Ones to look at may be such stocks as Bethlehem Steel, Blaw-Knox, Lone Star Cement, Weyerhaeuser Lumber, etc.

10

the calumet copper swing

In the spring of 1966 there developed a powerful international squeeze in copper. The use of copper in the electric and electronic industries in all nations was at an all-time high. As an alloy in copper and brass fabrication, and in coinage, the metal had a powerful global demand. Add to that the military demands, especially for use in brass cartridges and shells, and surging demands from copper-short nations such as Japan, and you can see how scarcities in the metal were building up. Finally, in the spring of 1966, there were strikes in the mines of Chile and Zambia (two of the world's major sources of the metal) which curtailed production. Thus copper was one of the hottest of metals. American consumption alone for 1966 was projected at 2.4 million tons—250,000 tons more than domestic output. Quotations in the metal in April, 1966, were bizarre. The U. S. domestic production was pegged at 36 cents a pound; foreign producers were quoting 42 cents; while the London Metal Exchange "free market" prices ranged above 80 cents; and in early April, Chile announced its intention to raise its export price from 42 to 62 cents a pound effective July 1.

Against this background of extraordinary demand, some remarkable developments were taking place in a long-established domestic company, Calumet & Hecla, Inc. This substantial copper producer and fabricator had just about run out of ore in its mines in northern Michigan and had been searching energetically for new ore sources to feed and supply its busy and profitable manufacturing division, Wolverine Tube. While the stock of Calumet & Hecla had been favorably considered as the equity of an efficient metal fabricator, nobody regarded it as an ore-rich property—not, at least, until April 6, 1966.

REPORTED STRIKE

After the stock closed on NYSE that day at

$38.50 (till then, the high for the year), the company announced a copper-ore discovery on Michigan's Keweenaw Peninsula, estimated at more than 35 million tons, grading in excess of 1.5 percent copper. (This means 30 pounds of copper to the ton of ore, and is relatively rich, as many mines mill ore assaying 10 pounds or less.) This announcement, related to the hottest copper market in history, created a market stampede in Calumet & Hecla common. The stock, which had closed at $38.50 on Wednesday, April 6, did not open the following day (April 7). Orders to buy "at the market" that Thursday were for 80,000 shares more than the sell orders; and there were only 2,123,410 shares of Calumet outstanding! The NYSE management stated officially: "In the ordinary situation of this kind the exchange specialist, in consultation with the floor governor, establishes a wide bid and offer quotation, considerably above the last sale, with a view to establishing a more realistic balance between buy and sell orders. In this very unusual instance, however, the imbalance is so excessive that the floor governors haven't as yet been able to determine what a fair bid and offer quotation should be."

Accordingly, Calumet didn't open for six days! Finally, on Friday, April 15, Calumet resumed trading at 1:22 P.M. with an initial block of 113,000 shares on the tape at $58.00 a share. After twenty minutes of frantic trading wherein 160,400 shares changed hands, trading was again halted and closed for the day at $63.50, up $25 a share from the closing price on April 6.

On Monday, April 18, Calumet & Hecla announced its first-quarter earnings, up 36 percent for the 1966 period, and equal to 77 cents a share, against 55 cents for the earlier year. This attracted further interest in the issue and, after a delayed opening on April 18, 201,600 shares traded in less than three hours. The stock closed at $61.50, down $2 from the record high of $63.50 established three days earlier.

A VALUABLE EXAMPLE

The reason for going into such detail about this Calumet & Hecla market binge is that it is without precedent in history. Further, it has an important message and lesson for stock traders. It illustrates forcibly what can happen to a stock with a relatively small number of shares outstanding, and a thin floating supply, when official good news is made public. This is not to suggest that a frantic purchase at $63.50 was prudent. On the contrary, perceptive investors should have been looking at this stock earlier, around the $30 level. It would have been possible considerably in advance to learn (1) that Calumet was shy of ore resources and searching energetically for new ones, (2) that a large new source, if found, might have a dramatic effect on share prices, and (3) that copper fabricating in a semiwar economy is a thriving business anyway and that Calumet's earnings were on the rise. Positions taken a month before the fireworks started would have delivered our target percentage for gain, 100 percent. Some advance inklings, moreover, might have been found in the rising volume in Calumet trading a few weeks before the publicized ore strike. Despite the proper insistence of SEC on prompt public presentation of important facts, without earlier benefits to "insiders" from prior knowledge of same, it must be obvious that exploration for ore bodies does not take place overnight. Someone is bound to know about it in advance — the company geologist, the exploration crew, top company officials and legal counsel, and secretaries who type the memos that describe, or record, details of the search for minerals. It would be incredible if this choice and valuable corporate information did not leak or trickle out somewhere along the line; and probably at least a few days before the strike became a headline in *The Wall Street Journal.* Out of every five human beings, one is a blabbermouth.

The moral of this story is to be on the lookout for good companies with smart managements that strive to correct shortages in vital raw materials. Then, by watching activity in the company's shares and by discreet inquiry, you may learn that something important is going on in the company. Such a research and observation program would have served you well in the case of Texas Gulf Sulphur, Banff Oil, Pine Point Mines, Molybdenum Corp., as well as Calumet.

Speculative opportunities in mineral companies are always in the making. It is up to you to find them, document them, and have the courage to act on significant information you may have unearthed. Happiness may be a hot metal stock.

11

the importance of leverage

While the stated objective of this book is to develop methods for selection of stocks that can double, it is quite possible to double your money in the market even when the stocks you buy advance less than 100 percent in price. The techniques for doing this come under the general head of leverage.

Leverage, simply stated, is getting somebody else's money to work for you. If properly understood and intelligently applied, leverage can notably accelerate and enhance your market gains. You acquire leverage in two ways: (1) by borrowing money to buy securities, or (2) by investing in companies with built-in leverage due to the existence of large amounts of senior securities ahead of their common stock. Leverage magnifies market swings, up or down.

LEVERAGE THROUGH BORROWED MONEY

Assume that you are convinced that Exotic Electronics at $50 a share is likely to advance swiftly. You wish to buy 100 shares costing $5,000 (excluding commission). Suppose, however, that you don't have $5,000 and must borrow part of the money if you buy this stock. If you do this through your broker, it is called buying on margin. Under current regulations, you must put up not less than 70 percent of the money needed, and the broker will then lend you the balance (30 percent) at an agreed rate of interest, say 6.25 percent. In this case, your real investment is not $5,000 but only $3,500 (70 percent of the total); and when and if Exotic Electronics sells at 85, you will have doubled your money ($5,000 plus $3,500) even though the stock itself did not double in price. The margin requirement has varied widely over the years. When it was 50 percent, all you would have needed to put up, in the example given, would have been $2,500, and your money would have doubled when Exotic hit 75.

These margin rates are determined by the

Federal Reserve Board; and they are changed fairly frequently in response to economic and credit conditions. If the Federal Reserve Board concludes that market speculation is being overdone, it will usually raise margin require-ments—even to 100 percent, or all cash! At slack periods in the economy, the permissible rate has been as low as 40 percent. In 1929, the rate was not regulated at all; and it was common practice for people, often with small resources, to buy stocks with as little as 10 percent down!

Although buying on margin (borrowing money) substantially increases potentials for gain on the dollars you invest, this leverage is a two-edged sword. Taking Exotic Electronics again, if after you bought the stock on a 50 percent margin at 50, the stock fell to 25, your $2,500 (margin) would have been wiped out; and long before the stock reached that point, your broker would surely have asked you for more money. Such a request, called a margin call, is always most disquieting, and many seasoned speculators make it a point never to respond. They prefer to let the broker sell them out and to take their loss rather than "follow a losing hand."

SUBSCRIPTION BORROWING

Even when margins are high, as currently at 70 percent, there may be some loopholes avail-able. One is the purchase of new stock on sub-scription rights. Each year many substantial

companies offer to their shareholders the right
to buy additional stock, in ratio to shares already
held, at a price somewhat below the market
quotation of the issue at the time. While many
stockholders may exercise these rights, others
may prefer not to put up additional money; so
they sell their rights and others buy them and
subscribe. Whether, in the above situations,
the stockholder, or someone else, subscribes to
the new stock, NYSE member firms will handle
the subscription for 25 percent down, and will
loan their customers the balance; they will carry
the account on that basis, unless (and until) the
stock declines substantially. In that event, you
will be asked to post more margin, or you will be
sold out. This broker-lending on "subscription"
stock applies equally in regard to stockholders'
rights to subscribe to new issues of convertible
preferred stocks or bonds.

Utility companies quite commonly, and industrial and financial companies less frequently,
offer subscription rights to their shareholders.
As a typical example, a company's stock is selling at $50, and the company offers its share-
holders the right to purchase new common stock
at $40 a share, in ratio of 1 new share for each
10 shares held. Since it takes 10 "rights" to
buy 1 new share, each "right" to purchase at
$40 is theoretically worth about $1. The holder
of 1,000 shares of the subject common stock
may thus add 100 shares to his holdings by putting up $4,000; or he can sell his 1,000 "rights"
at $1 each and realize $1,000. If, however, he

decides to subscribe through his brokerage firm, he need put up only $1,000; and the broker will supply the other $3,000 as above outlined.

BANK BORROWING

Another way to create leverage is to borrow from your bank instead of from your broker when you buy securities. This technique can be just a little devious, because banks, in lending to those buying stocks, are supposed to follow the same regulations as brokerage firms, and relate the percentage of the loan to the margin requirements prevailing at the time. A bank, however, may extend to an individual with excellent credit a loan on signature alone, or a loan on collateral, with the purpose of the loan allegedly to meet some other financial need than the purchase of securities for speculative gain. In such cases, and without full or accurate disclosure by the borrower as to the real purpose of the loan, the bank may actually lend on no collateral at all or by advancing as much as 70 percent of the market value of collateral offered. The net effect of this is that you borrow at 30 percent or less and create a leverage for your dollars of more than 2 to 1.

LEVERAGE FROM CAPITAL STRUCTURES

Another way of maximizing the gaining power (leverage) of your dollars does not involve borrowing money; it involves investment in the common stocks of companies that are themselves highly leveraged by large amounts of senior securities (bonds or preferred stock) placed ahead of common stock in the corporate structure. For example, a representative electric utility may be capitalized 50 percent in bonds, 20 percent in preferred stock, and 30 percent in common. Here again the investment leverage on the common is better than 2 to 1. As an example of leverage, ahead of the 37.3 million common shares of Consolidated Edison Company are $5 million in preferred stock, and $1,786 million in long-term debt. New York Central Railroad has $802 million in debt, ahead of its 6.9 million shares of common stock outstanding. Since all net earnings remaining after payment of interest go to stockholders, the leverage created by debt can generate dramatic gains in per-share earnings in a prosperous company.

CONVERTIBLES AND WARRANTS

Other leveraged securities are convertible preferred stocks and bonds, and warrants. Convertible securities are generally preceded by other debt. For speculation, they are safer than common stocks because they are senior securities; they pay a regular interest or dividend return; and they usually enjoy active trading markets. They offer substantial opportunities for gain, however, because they can be converted into common stock of the same company at a certain price for a certain period of time, defined in the bond indenture and in the prospectus offering the securities.

An illustration will help. Crowell-Collier 4.5 percent debentures, due 1981, are convertible into the common stock at 40. At the time this was written, (Jan. 11, 1967) Crowell-Collier common was selling at 44 — above the conversion figure. Without a conversion feature, a Crowell-Collier 4.5 percent debenture would have sold at around 90; converted into stock, its value was $1,100 (44 x 25). Because of the conversion privilege, however, these bonds were selling at 125. In the belief that Crowell common would continue to go up, investors were willing to pay $150 for the bond-conversion privilege. In this convertible, you have, at your wish, either a $1,000 bond or 25 shares of common stock; and for every advance in the price of the common, the bond will theoretically advance $25, or 2 1/2 points. The conversion value creates a leveraged investment, a leverage that can be further increased if you borrow part of the money to buy the bond.

There are dozens of convertible bonds to choose from; and over two hundred different issues of convertible preferred stocks in the market today. Representative issues would include:

CONVERTIBLE BONDS

ISSUE	RATE	MATURITY	CURRENT CONVERSION PRICE
Air Reduction	3 7/8	1987	58
Olin Mathieson	5 1/2	1982	60 1/2
Virginia Electric Power	3 5/8	1986	51

PREFERRED STOCKS

		CONVERTIBLE INTO
Atlantic Richfield	3	.85 share of common
Continental Oil	2	.73 share of common
Transamerica	4.50	3.69 shares of common

In consideration of convertible securities for speculative purchase, there are six main points to keep in mind: (1) it generally pays to buy a convertible when it is first available, before the issue has attracted a wide interest among investors; (2) buy the convertible bond or preferred at a price as close as possible to the price at which it would sell if it carried no conversion privilege; (3) seek as long a conversion period as possible; (4) note its call prices and terms — an early-redemption provision is often used by companies to compel conversion of an issue; (5) make sure that the issuing company is a profitable and rapidly growing one, so that the subject common may perform well market-wise, and thus propel the price of the "convert" upward; and (6) prefer large, active, listed issues.

To indicate the potentials for gain among convertibles, as of Jan. 11, 1967, Metromedia Broadcasting convertible 6's due 1975 at 265; Xerox 4's due 1984 at 231; Ling-Temco-Vought 5 3/4's due 1976 at 280; and United Aircraft 4 1/2's due 1988 at 260. All of these were originally available in the market at slight premiums over par. Lively ones now on the scene might be Occidental Petroleum 5 1/4's due 1991, General Time 4 3/4's due 1979, Reynolds Metals 4 1/2's due 1991, Dresser Industries 4 1/8's due 1977.

It is possible for a dynamic "convert" to rise by 100 percent in a single year, stimulated both by the leverage created by the capital structure of the issuing company and by the further leverage built up by all the money invested by buyers of the related common, whose buying power tends to drive the stock upward.

WARRANTS

The wildest corporate security is the warrant. It is the will-o'-the-wisp of finance. It represents no ownership in, or claim on, assets or earnings; it has no book value and never pays dividends. Yet it represents the most leveraged type of security and, under the right conditions, can produce fabulous capital gains. A warrant permits the holder to profit from the rise of a company's common stock by using far fewer dollars than would be needed to purchase actual shares (warrants always sell for less than the related stocks). Warrants illustrate the adage "The farther out on a dog's tail, the wider the swing!" Gains of 3,000 or 5,000 percent have been recorded. Atlas Corporation perpetual warrants, for example, rose from 25 cents each in 1942 to $12.50 in 1946. Warrants, being preceded by every other security in a corporation's financial structure, possess unique leverage and enable $1 to do the work of many in a lively stock market. Equally, warrants can decline sensationally, and become totally worthless if not exercised before their expiration dates.

Essentially, a warrant is just a contract whereby a company agrees to sell to the holder of the warrant shares a share, or fraction thereof, of its common stock at a specified price (or range of prices), usually with a certain time limit, after which the warrant expires. (A few warrants are perpetual.) When speculating in warrants, the time factor is thus all-important. Ideally, warrants should be purchased in the early stages of bull markets, when the subscription price specified in the warrant is substantially below the prevailing quotation for the subject stock. Warrants are prophetic investments, and they almost always sell at far more than they are intrinsically worth. For example, on January 5, 1967, Atlas Corporation warrants, each permitting purchase of a share of Atlas common at $6.25 (without time limit) sold at $1.75 each; yet they were then without any actual value, since Atlas common sold on that day, and was actively trading, at only $3.

Interesting and possibly gainful warrants for you to consider are:

REPRESENTATIVE WARRANTS

COMPANY	RIGHT TO BUY ONE SHARE AT	EXPIRATION DATE
Alleghany	$ 3.75	Perpetual
Atlas	6.25	Perpetual
Trans World Airlines	20.00	12/1/73
Tri-Continental	See note [1]	Perpetual
Pacific Petroleums	19.00	3/1/68
Uris Buildings	See note [2]	5/1/75

NOTES
[1] Right to buy 1.27 shares at $17.76 per share
[2] Right to buy 1.0609 shares at $11.78 each

Warrants are the riskiest and raciest corporate security. As a vehicle for swift trading gains involving relatively small amounts of capital, they are without a rival. They can, in some instances, advance three times as fast as the common in the same company; and they can plummet like a dive-bomber. But they belong on the shopping list of everyone interested in doubling his money.

This chapter may be one you will wish to refer to with some frequency, because leverage in any form is a most important ingredient in any successful formula for stock speculation. It's always delightful, and often rewarding, to have other people's money working for you!

12

doublers on new york and american stock exchanges 1961-64

This chapter is designed to develop market judgment by observation of past market actions. We have set down here lists of those issues on the New York Stock Exchange and the American Stock Exchange that doubled in the years 1961 through 1964. The purpose of listing winners in these years is to highlight the kinds of stocks that can score important gains; and to note that, in certain years, gainful speculation is quite difficult. For example, 1962 was a year of across-the-board declines on both the New York and the American Exchanges. Net advances were rare oases in a downward desert. Had we sought to double our money in that year, the best way would have been to sell short.

NEW YORK STOCK EXCHANGE ISSUES
THAT DOUBLED IN 1961

STOCK	FIRST SALE OF YEAR	LAST SALE OF YEAR
Amerace	15 5/8*	31 3/8
American Enka	20 1/8	45 1/4
E. W. Bliss	16 5/8	34 1/4
Century Industries	10	19 5/8 (almost)
Cooper Tire & Rubber	7 3/8	15
Crown Cork & Seal	42 3/4	129
Dunhill International	9 bid	22 3/4
W. R. Grace	35 1/2	82 3/4
Granby Mining	6 1/2	18 1/8
Grayson Robinson Stores (Later merged)	8 1/4	24 1/2
Great Western Financial	31 7/8	62 1/2 (almost; sold below 10 in 1966)
Kayser-Roth	13	25 5/8 (almost)
Loew's Theatres	16	42 3/4
MCA	37 5/8	79
National Cash Register	62 1/2	131 3/4
Northwest Airlines	15 7/8	32 (a real swinger)

*Adjusted for 3-for-1 split.

STOCK	FIRST SALE OF YEAR	LAST SALE OF YEAR
Philadelphia & Reading	34	79 7/8
Ronson	13	26 1/8
San Diego Imperial	7 5/8	15 1/2
Stokely-Van Camp	16 7/8	33 7/8
Tandy	4 1/8	11 3/8
John R. Thompson	10 1/8	24
U. S. Industries	9 1/8	21 1/8
Ward Foods	6 1/4	15 5/8
Warner Brothers Pictures	17	33 7/8 (almost)

AMERICAN STOCK EXCHANGE ISSUES THAT DOUBLED IN 1961

STOCK	FIRST SALE OF YEAR	LAST SALE OF YEAR
Associates Testing Labs	14 1/4	28 1/4
Barton's Candy	5 1/2	16 1/2
A. S. Beck	10	19 3/4 (almost)
Budget Finance	7 1/2	16 5/8
Canadian Industrial Gas & Oil	3 15/16	8
Christiana Oil	3 1/2	8 3/8
Cinerama	5 1/8	19 7/8
Clayton & Lambert	7 1/8	15 (bid)
Continental Materials	3/8	2 1/8
DeJay Stores	2	8 7/8
Detroit Industrial Gas	5 1/8	10 7/8
Dome Petroleum	6 3/4	14 1/2
Duro-Test	27 1/2	60 1/2
Electronic Specialty	13 7/8	27 5/8
Federated Resources	5 7/8	12 3/4
Financial General	9 3/4	20 1/8
General Gas	5	11 3/8
Great Lakes Chemical	2	4 7/8
Gulf States Land & Industries	11	21 3/4 (almost)

STOCK	FIRST SALE OF YEAR	LAST SALE OF YEAR
Gulf & Western Industries	10 1/4	34
H & B American	1 3/4	3 3/4
Hebrew National Kosher Foods	3 3/4	11 5/8
Helmerich & Payne	7 3/4	16 3/4
Hill's Supermarkets	10	26 1/2
Hoffman International	3 7/8	8 1/2
Holly Corp.	4 1/8	19 1/8
S. Klein Department Stores	12 1/2	26 3/4
Klion (H. L.)	3 7/8	8 3/4
Mount Clemens Metal Products	2 1/8 (bid)	14
Napco Industries	3 3/4	8 7/8
Occidental Petroleum	4 3/4	25
Old Town	3 7/8	13 5/8
Pep Boys	7 5/8	24 1/2
Quebec Lithium	2 5/16	4 5/8
Rayette (Later merged)	7 1/8	18 1/2
Royal American Industries	2	4 1/8
Royalite Oil	6 1/8	12 1/4
Russeks Fifth Ave.	2 1/4	4 7/8
Ryerson & Haynes	1 7/8 (bid)	4 3/8
Southern Calif. Petroleum	7 1/8 (bid)	16 7/8
Standard-Thomson	3 3/4	8 1/8
Steel Parts	8	24 3/4
Tower Acceptance	4	11 7/8
Webb & Knapp	1	2 1/4
R. C. Williams	4	16
Wood Newspaper Machinery	7 7/8	15 7/8

1962 DOUBLERS ON NYSE

STOCK	FIRST SALE OF YEAR	LAST SALE OF YEAR
Consolidated Cigar	21 7/8*	49 3/4

*Adjusted for 3-for-1 split.

1962 DOUBLERS ON ASE

STOCK	FIRST SALE OF YEAR	LAST SALE OF YEAR
Simca Automobiles	16	44 1/2 (bid)

1963 DOUBLERS ON NYSE

STOCK	FIRST SALE OF YEAR	LAST SALE OF YEAR
Bulova Watch	9 7/8	26
Chicago & North Western	13 1/4	25 1/2 (almost double)
Chrysler	18 3/8*	42
Dr. Pepper	21 1/2 (bid)	49 7/8
Evans Products	9 1/2	20 1/8
Haveg Industries	19 7/8	39 (almost)
Monon Railroad, Class B	9 3/8	29 7/8
Northwest Airlines	37 7/8	73 1/2
Pan American World Airways	21 3/8	52 1/2
St. Joseph Lead	25 1/4	51 1/4
Shahmoon Industries	9 1/2	19 1/2
Western Air Lines	31 3/4	73
Xerox	31 1/4†	85

1963 DOUBLERS ON ASE

STOCK	FIRST SALE OF YEAR	LAST SALE OF YEAR
Atlas Consolidated Mining & Development	6 7/8	14 5/8
Bunker Hill	8 3/4	22 1/2
Carey Baxter & Kennedy	4 (bid)	9

*Adjusted price. Chrysler had two 2-for-1 splits in 1963.
†Adjusted for 5-for-1 split.

STOCK	FIRST SALE OF YEAR	LAST SALE OF YEAR
Dennison Manufacturing, Class A	19	54 1/4
Falcon Seaboard Drilling	4 3/8 (bid)	14 1/2
Felmont Oil	5 1/4	10 3/8 (almost)
Guerdon Industries	3 1/2	7 5/8
Gulf States Land & Industries	14 3/4	28 3/4
Kin-Ark Oil	1 5/8	4 1/8
Mount Clemens Metal Products	5 7/8	13 7/8
New Process	38 7/8	80 1/2
Philips Electronics & Pharmaceuticals	25	55 3/8
Pyle National	26 1/8	65 3/4
Rayette	23 1/4	46 (almost)
San Carlos Milling	7 1/4 (bid)	14 (almost)
Silicon Transistor	4 3/8	11
Syntex	12*	125
Technicolor	8 3/4	18 5/8
Zapata Off-Shore	4 3/4 (bid)	9 7/8

1964 DOUBLERS ON NYSE

STOCK	FIRST SALE OF YEAR	LAST SALE OF YEAR
Braniff Airways	13	27 3/4
Bucyrus-Erie	19 5/8	39 3/8
Chicago & North Western	25 7/8	57 7/8
Evans Products	21 5/8	42 3/4
Fluor	16	35
I-T-E Circuit Breaker	17 1/2	38
Pan American Sulphur	20 3/4	44 7/8
Sunshine Mining	10 7/8	25 3/8
Texas Gulf Sulphur	24 1/8	51 1/8

*Adjusted for 3-for-1 split.

1964 DOUBLERS ON ASE

STOCK	FIRST SALE OF YEAR	LAST SALE OF YEAR
Acme Missiles & Const.	2	7 1/4
Aeronca	2 1/4	6 1/8
Allied Paper	6 3/4	13 7/8
Alloys Unlimited	4 3/8	13 1/8
APL	5 1/4	11 1/8
Berkey Photo	9 1/2	19 3/8
Brazilian Traction (Now Brazilian Light & Power)	2 3/8	4 7/8
Data-Control Systems	24 1/2	56 1/4
Day Mines	5 1/8	10 3/4
Driver-Harris	17 1/2 (bid)	35 1/2
Fotochrome	2	9 1/4
Fresnillo	6 3/4	13 5/8
Greer Hydraulics	2 1/2	12 1/8
Holly Corp.	9 1/4	23
International Products	3 7/8	15 1/4
D. Kaltman	1 3/8	4 1/2
Kin-Ark Oil	4 1/4	9 1/4
Lee Filter	2	5 1/8
Magellan Petroleum	13/16	4
Missouri-Kansas-Texas Cert.	5	15 1/8
Norfolk Southern	12 1/2	30
Old Town	8 3/8	38 3/8
Pantasote	3 1/4	7
Rollins Inc.	16 3/4	76 1/4
Savoy Industries	8 3/4	30
Unexcelled Inc.	6 3/4	26 1/4
Unishops	9 3/4	21 1/8

1961

Taking up the lists chronologically twenty-five issues doubled in 1961 on the Big Board. Theatrical shares were perhaps most noteworthy, with Loew's, MCA, and Warner Bros. doubling. The year was a big one also for savings-and-loan companies, especially Great Western and San Diego Imperial. (By 1966, they were in deep doldrums, however.) Apart from these bracketings, the gains were in quite unrelated industries and seemed to be generated more by merger-minded companies, such as Philadelphia & Reading, W. R. Grace, U. S. Industries, and Ward Foods; and by aggressive merchandisers, such as Kayser-Roth, Grayson Robinson, and National Cash Register. Certain stocks caught random speculative fancy — Northwest Airlines, Granby, Ronson, and American Enka. Mergers, movies, and merchants were the favored speculations of 1961.

On the American Stock Exchange, forty-six issues doubled in 1961. Many of these were stocks of young companies, with unusually high growth rates. To illustrate, the earnings growth rates of Occidental Petroleum, Barton's Candy, Rayette, and Pep Boys were quite spectacular. Electronic Specialty expanded its earnings swiftly, and gained a junior glamour rating; Gulf & Western was beginning to display its genius for gain by merger; Hebrew National had just gone public and investors for the first time could acquire this unique equity in the market. It was also a good year for merchandising, so that Hill's Supermarkets, S. Klein Department Stores, Pep Boys, Russeks 5th Avenue, and De-Jay Stores prospered. Natural resources were popular, too, accounting for the interest in Christiana Oil, Dome Petroleum, Canadian Industrial Gas, Royalite Oil, and General Gas.

The year 1961 was marked by the great volume of new stock issues offered (over $1 billion) so that speculative interest was seething. In fact, in 1961, if you dabbled in speculations, quality was not an essential ingredient for success. Many shares went ahead purely on mass popularity and psychology, unmindful of fundamentals, good or bad. Typical zoomers on general principles were Cinerama, Tower Acceptance, and Webb & Knapp.

1962

This year, as mentioned earlier, was a dreary one for avid traders, and had this book come out in June, 1962, it would have languished. In midsummer of that year, people weren't very confident that any stock could ever double!

1963

The year 1963 was a rebound year. Sentiment, which was so gloomy in mid-1962 (after the market had fallen 30 percent in six months), turned confident, and many issues rose not so much because of notable advances in earning power as because they had been hammered down below their worth a year earlier. The lively uptick was far more visible on the ASE than on the Big Board, however. On the NYSE, the sensational performers were two rails (Chicago & North Western and Monon Railroad, Class B) and three airlines (Pan American,

Northwest, and Western). Xerox Corporation, one of the few stocks to be a market darling for several years in a row, attained virtuosity in 1963. In Xerox, the propellants were the dynamics of the copy-machine industry and the solid industrial leadership and rapid rise in earnings of the company (accompanied by stock splits); and significant buying by certain institutions.

On the ASE, the year 1963 turned the spotlight of interest onto offshore oil drilling, with 100 percent gains by Falcon Seaboard and Zapata Off-Shore. Metals were favored, too. Atlas Consolidated and Bunker Hill moved ahead in price, and both companies gained notably in corporate stature. Other issues scored well in response to substantial growth in earning power: Rayette, Dennison Manufacturing, and New Process Company. Finally, Syntex moved sensationally, reporting a tenfold gain.

1964

During 1964, there was no market basket full of winners on the NYSE — only nine. They included an airline, Braniff; two construction-industry entries, Bucyrus-Erie and Fluor Corporation; a volatile industrial, Evans Products; Sunshine Mining, with a silver lining; and Texas Gulf Sulphur, which had a mixed blessing (SEC investigation) in its big copper strike at Timmins, Ontario.

The list of double gainers on ASE was substantial — twenty-seven. Stellar performers were

Brazilian Traction, the billion-dollar electric-light-and-power company in Brazil; Data-Control Systems, a leader in automation; Magellan Petroleum, scoring on an oil strike in Australia; and technical companies — Acme Missiles, Greer Hydraulics, Lee Filter, Alloys Unlimited, and Unexcelled Inc. Two railroads made the scene — Norfolk Southern and Missouri-Kansas-Texas certificates. This seemed to be more of a year for special speculative situations than any majestic upward price march stimulated primarily by earning power.

The years 1961-64 illustrate our thesis quite well. In every year when markets are strong, a significant number of stocks will double in value, and unusual increases in per-share earnings are the commonest and most dependable motivating forces. Equally, in bear or depressed markets, even issues with very good earnings and golden prospects have a hard time bucking the tide, and doublers are few.

13

big swings on the big board in 1965 and 1966

The New York Stock Exchange lists about 1,240 issues of common stock, and these include the equities of some of the largest, most famous companies in the world. There is AT&T, with 538 million shares of stock outstanding; General Motors, with 286 million; and other giant blue chips such as U. S. Steel, Sears, Roebuck, Standard Oil of New Jersey, Texaco, Swift & Company, and Pacific Gas & Electric. But the shares of titanic enterprises, as you will note

141

from the tabulations that follow, while trading in great volume, are seldom dazzling performers or dramatic movers within any short period of time. In fact, in our search for annual doublers, we must almost rule out the shares of the two hundred largest corporations. It's uncommon for any one of them to move widely in a hurry, first, because they have so many millions of shares outstanding and, second, because they already have such huge earnings that it would be most unusual for one of them to increase its net profits within a single year by as much as 50 percent. (Rising earnings or the expectations of them are the most powerful underlying market propellants.) So the first principle we can set down in advance is this: if you seek a 100 percent gain within a year, don't buy shares in the biggest companies. Look over the feature gainers for 1965 and you'll see that it's among the second and third echelons of companies that the biggest swings on the Big Board occur.

The year 1965 was a fine and representative bull-market year, in which there were fifty-five issues on the Big Board that doubled. Our definition of a doubler, in any year, is a stock that on the last trading day of the subject year was selling at least twice as high as it sold on the first business day in January. Actually, this arbitrarily restricts the list, because a number of stocks that do not qualify on this basis actually doubled in price some time during the year, and several stocks that did so were unable to hold their gain until the year end.

In any event, 1965 was an excellent year in which to test our theories. Here is the list of January-to-December doublers, with comment on the group and certain individual performances following directly thereafter:

NYSE DOUBLERS

STOCK	FIRST SALE OF YEAR	LAST SALE OF YEAR
Admiral Corporation	15 3/4	65
Allied Products	10 1/4	35
American Ship Building	13	26 1/4
Bangor Punta Alegre Sugar	15 1/8	32 1/2
Boston & Maine	10 1/2	23 3/4
Braniff Airways	27 5/8	72 7/8
Burndy	15 5/8	46
Burroughs Corporation	25	49 7/8
Chemetron	27 1/4	57 7/8
Chicago & North Western	58 1/2	121
Collins Radio	19 1/2	49 1/4
Colt Industries	12	23 5/8
Congoleum-Nairn	15 1/2	35 7/8
Consolidated Freight-ways (Moved from OTC during year)	19 1/2 (OTC)	44 1/4
Continental Air Lines	20	52 7/8
Continental Copper & Steel	7 7/8	22 3/4
Crescent	10 1/8	19 7/8
CTS	25 7/8	59
Delta Air Lines	30 7/8*	71 1/2
Douglas Aircraft	29 1/4	74 5/8
Eastern Air Lines	42 1/2	89

*Adjusted figure. Split 2 for 1, November, 1965.

STOCK	FIRST SALE OF YEAR	LAST SALE OF YEAR
Emerson Radio & Phonograph	10 3/8	22
Fairchild Camera & Instrument	27 3/4	150 1/2
Fairchild Hiller	9 1/8	18
Fansteel Metallurgical	10 3/8	20 1/8
Gulf & Western Industries	31 1/2	92 7/8
Holiday Inns of America	16 3/8	31 5/8
International Rectifier	7 1/4	18 1/8
IRC	14 1/8	29 5/8
Lehigh Valley Industries	2 1/4	8 1/4
Ling-Temco-Vought	17 3/4	48 1/4
Litton Industries	74 7/8	139*
Lukens Steel	20 5/8*	53 1/8
Magnavox	31 3/4	81 7/8
Motorola	95 1/2	164 1/2
National Airlines	34**	70 1/4
New Jersey Zinc	23	49
Northwest Airlines	63 1/4	127 5/8
Pittsburgh Coke & Chemical	20 1/2	49 1/8
Polaroid	45 7/8	116 5/8
Rohr	18 7/8	42 1/4
Ryan Aeronautical	9 1/16**	17 3/4
Sangomo Electric	10 3/8	30
SCM	17 1/2	53 1/2
Spartans Industries	16 3/4	39 1/2
Standard Kollsman Industries	8 5/8	23 1/8
Union Carbide	29 3/8	68 1/2
United Aircraft Corporation	21 7/8***	82 1/8
Varian Associates	13 1/8	26 5/8
Victor Comptometer	15 3/8	33 1/2
Vornado	30 3/8	68 3/4

*Split 2-for-1 in December. Old common shown.
**Adjusted 2-for-1 split.   ***Adjusted 3-for-1 split.

STOCK	FIRST SALE OF YEAR	LAST SALE OF YEAR
Ward Foods	6 7/8	16 3/4
White Consolidated Industries	18	48 3/4
Xerox	99	202
Zenith Radio	63 1/2	121 1/4

COMMENT ON 1965 NYSE DOUBLERS

The year 1965 was a flowering one for speculators on NYSE. There were fifty-five winners (by our standards) and they appeared in almost every category. First of all, the year was a general boom year—in motorcars, construction, merchandising, utilities, finance, metals, mining, rails, airlines, and Gross National Product. The year seemed a safe and promising one, and more stockholders and speculators were on the scene than at any time in history. It was thus to be expected that trader confidence was bubbling, and that speculation would spread across the Board to include almost any stock of merit and motion. Also, many issues traded in probably greater volume than ever before—Eastern Air Lines, Chicago & North Western, Fairchild Camera, Polaroid, Motorola, SCM, and Admiral, for example. This was the year of the "performance" stocks—issues with wide popular appeal and notable rises in earnings that attracted heavy mutual-fund buying for speculative gain. The point was brought forcibly home to all perceptive investors and traders that stocks could swing lustily up and down from day to day, with these swings quite unaccounted for by any specific improvement or deterioration in the welfare of the subject companies.

In other words, in substantial companies with a popular appeal, such as SCM, Xerox, Syntex, supply-demand factors might well dictate price changes — and they did! Issues with the smallest floating supplies frequently performed best, and several stocks were pushed up simply because buyers day after day outnumbered sellers. Add to this built-up individual clamor for particular issues the frequent buy orders, in 5,000 to 50,000 lots, by the funds, and you can understand how there developed a mass-market psychology that was roaringly bullish, and that carried many issues to alpine levels found to be quite untenable a year later.

This list of NYSE 1965 leaders should be studied quite carefully by speculators. In particular, it would be useful to look up the percentage of outstanding shares of an issue traded in the course of a year. It is an observable phenomenon in bull markets that sharp increase in volume in an active issue is usually accompanied by rising prices. For this reason, many successful speculators watch the volume of trading in individual issues like hawks; and when they see a stock suddenly trading in twice its accustomed volume and rising on this volume, they buy. They do so often without bothering to look up the fundamental data — earnings, dividends, profit margins, growth rates, etc. Such traders believe the secret of market success lies in riding stocks in active market motion rather than in waiting for improved earnings to be slowly reflected in the price of a stock with a meager market following.

The year also illustrated another important point useful for speculators — the advantage of trading in "hot" industries. In 1965, nearly all analysts, economists, and investment services were convinced that air transportation had come of age; that the high costs of converting from "props" to jets had been assimilated; and that airlines would now make money as they began to fill all the new seating-capacity acquired. Speculators throughout the land "bought" this theory of airline prosperity — and look at the stock gains that resulted in a single year! Braniff, Continental, Delta, Eastern, National, Northwest — all more than doubled, with a related gain in United Aircraft, largest builder of jet engines.

Following further this "popular industry" theory, look at TV in 1965! People were convinced that color TV was about to really "take over," so traders swarmed all over Admiral (which quadrupled in price), Collins, Emerson, Magnavox, Motorola, and Zenith. Just think of this: if, in January, 1965, you had become convinced that only two industries were then worth speculating in, and forthwith purchased all the TV and airline issues cited in the previous paragraphs, you would have owned twelve stocks that doubled — and nobody would have done better than that! So start now picking the "hot" industry for 1967!

While the foregoing group of dramatic gainers is just what the doctor ordered for our purposes, note that these fifty-five issues that doubled are only 4.5 percent of all the issues listed on NYSE. Also, observe that the Dow-Jones Industrial Average — the most famous market barometer — displayed an average rise of only 10.88 percent for the full year. The issues on this list thus represent an elite group. In some way, and for a variety of reasons, this small list of stocks outperformed the whole market by a very wide margin. Let's try to see why some of these virtuosos performed so well, not as an historical exercise, but to observe from these standouts the particular qualities they possessed that made them so eagerly sought and bought. Are there certain vital ingredients common to all hot stocks? We think so.

POLAROID CORPORATION

Here's an obvious swinger! Widely talked about in board rooms from coast to coast, it qualifies as a "hot stock" by having risen in 1965 from a low of 44 to a high of 130. Possibly one of the reasons for the "action" was the very name of one of its leading products, the Swinger camera! Over 800,000 Model 20's were sold in 1965; and treble that in 1966.

Polaroid, renowned for excellence in instant and color photography, offered many facets of attraction to speculators: (1) the popularity of photography in a high-leisure, high-income society; (2) the lure of Polaroid's almost continuous improvements; (3) the rapid advance in earning, from 71 cents in 1963 to more than double that in 1965; (4) the steady "repeat" demand for film; (5) whispers about an exciting new TV tube and a novel copying machine; and (6) a pretax profit margin of above 27 percent.

It is hard to decide which of the foregoing plus factors were most influential in causing Polaroid to go up. It is to be observed, however, that together these elements produced a picture of profits, progress, and potential about Polaroid so attractive that, after drifting in lower price zones for four years, the stock broke away in 1965 and rewarded early buyers with market gains of well over 100 percent. This is an exciting picture, whether viewed from a slide rule or from a Polaroid lens! Finally, market motion was stimulated by belief that Polaroid would increase its sales by 30 percent plus in 1966. Polaroid in 1965 was a classic study in glamour and gain, with its stock undulating in a broad market terrain provided by 15,750,000 shares listed and traded on NYSE. Nobody knows whether Polaroid will repeat, but it was certainly an authentic market star in 1965.

NORTHWEST AIRLINES, INC.

This proved a most rewarding selection in 1965, moving from a low of 61 3/4 to a high of 142 1/2 (and still higher in 1966). What was the propulsion here? (1) A widely held belief that air transportation has come of age and that a long-term uptrend in traffic revenues and profits is now discernible; (2) the fact that Northwest was an elite selection within the industry on the basis of historic growth, excellence of management, taut cost controls, an ultramodern jet fleet, and some of the most desirable air routes in the world; (3) the upthrust in earnings from $5.86 a share in 1964 to an indicated $10 in 1965 and possibly $13 in 1966; and (4) the probability of higher dividends and a stock split.

The combination of these factors generated a powerful market following in NWA even though the stock orbited in a price range not generally popular. A review and acceptance of the four points listed above early in 1965 would have provided ample justification for speculative purchase, especially so because the whole airline group documented its popularity by heavy trading profits and exciting gains in other issues — Eastern, Braniff, National, Pan Am, etc. The real logic behind the purchase of NWA was that it was probably the choicest major stock in a surging industry.

SCM CORPORATION

Here was a real breakaway stock in 1965. Under its pre-1958 name of Smith-Corona Marchant, Inc., the company had turned in rather routine earnings and so-so market performance for a few years, when suddenly it "caught on."

The company, benefiting from vigorous topside direction under Mr. Emerson B. Mead, President, increased its sales by over 60 percent in six years, and in two years' time became the second largest producer (next to Xerox) of electrostatic copiers; and the only maker of electric portable typewriters. Plant capacity was greatly increased, and production costs significantly reduced by automation.

These elements were all important, but the clincher was the resultant sharp rise in earnings for fiscal 1965 (year ending June 30). Net income per share rose 57 percent to $1.47, against 83 cents a share in 1964. Because of the indigenous glamour of the business-machine industry (generated and sustained by IBM and Xerox) and SCM's dramatic advances within the industry in sales and profits, this stock became a hot one. Its earlier rise from 10 1/2 to over 20 in 1963-64 set the base and provided the launching pad for a driving gain in 1965, from a low of 16 1/4 to a high of 62 5/8 (well over 300 percent). During the year, 11,106,000 shares of SCM were traded—about four times its capitalization. Such a volume of trading, on the upside, is a usual characteristic of a breakaway stock.

ADMIRAL CORPORATION

One of the explosive industries of 1965 was color TV. After a decade of research, color tubes were improved, and new color sets, offered at somewhat lower prices, caught on big. Projections for 1965 indicated that, by the year's end, there would be 55 million homes with TV sets, but only 5.4 million with color sets. This pointed to a fantastic demand for future years, as color-TV ownership became a social compulsion, and as programs in color expanded to satisfy viewers and advertisers alike.

Color consoles thus became the "in" thing, in both suburbia and Wall Street, and the shares of the standout producers became market darlings. There was a surging board-room clamor for Zenith, Motorola, RCA, and Magnavox, but no issue generated a more ecstatic following than Admiral. It rose during the year from 16 to 56, although it paid no dividend; and it continued its spectacular rise well into 1966. Why was this? What were the propulsive forces behind Admiral? Sales and earnings, basically.

First-half sales in 1965 at Admiral were up 32 percent, and net earnings 61 percent! Sales, which were $238 million for the full year 1964, were expected to cross $280 million in 1965 (they did); and net earnings were expected to rise from $1.66 (1964) to above $2.50, and this after heavy charge-offs ($1 a share pretax) for entering color-tube manufacture. Admiral, which had been buying its spectrum tubes principally from National Video and Sylvania, decided to manufacture its own 25-inch color tubes beginning in 1965, and added 19-inch tubes in 1966. This was to ensure adequate supply and prompt deliveries, and incidentally to improve overall manufacturing profitability.

Not only were Admiral TV sales soaring, but its appliance business was zooming, particularly its Duplex two-door freezer-refrigerator with automatic ice-cube maker. Altogether, Admiral appeared on the threshold of dramatic gains in sales and profits running well into future years. There were unofficial estimates that Admiral might even duplicate its 1950 results, when the company earned $7.67 (prior to which the stock had also advanced several hundred percent).

Thus, in review, Admiral became a hot stock in 1965 because: (1) the company was astride the mainstream of consumer electronic demand — color TV; (2) it was producing attractive sets with increasing profit margins; (3) it was creating its own color-tube facility; (4) net profits might treble within three years; and (5) the company had a small capitalization (only 2,450,000 shares) with 40 percent owned by management, which resulted in a small floating supply of shares, always a powerful market force in hot stocks. Finally, there was the lingering memory, among older traders, of swift and extraordinary gains in Admiral in the 1948-50 period. Admiral is a copybook example of hot stock.

FAIRCHILD CAMERA & INSTRUMENT CORPORATION

The largest percentage rise in 1965 in any company shares listed on the Big Board was scored by Fairchild Camera. From 27 1/2 at the end of 1964, the stock closed in 1965 at 150 1/2, an advance of 447.3 percent. This standout performance may be attributed to four things: (1) romance, (2) a dazzling rise in sales and earnings, (3) a remarkable improvement in pretax margins, and (4) a relatively small share capitalization.

The romance was provided by Fairchild's leadership in the electronic field of integrated microcircuits; its cockpit voice recorder, now required on all jet aircraft; and its significant position in space and defense systems.

Early in 1965, analysts were convinced that Fairchild would surge ahead statistically — and it surely lived up to its billing. Sales rose 30 percent above 1964, and net earnings advanced dramatically from 75 cents (1964) to $3.25 in 1965. Pretax profit margins — 2.6 percent in the earlier year — were 9 percent in 1965, an impressive improvement and solid evidence of managerial excellence.

Capitalization (December 31, 1964) was $29.7 million in long-term debt, followed by only 2,556,657 shares of common. Proving the popularity of this stock, 10,017,900 shares changed hands in 1965 — four times the outstanding capital! When you see such volume in trading, on the up side in relation to shares outstanding, you almost certainly mark a hot stock with almost compulsive forward momentum. Earning projection for Fairchild for 1966 is over $5 a share, an excellent gain also, but not enough to make Fairchild common advance another 400 percent! Fairchild in 1965 had everything going for it!

Concluding our observations on 1965, the year was notable marketwise for its industry preferences, with airlines and TV hogging the spotlight. The year further illustrates well the influence of institutional buying of glamour and action stocks. In prior years, mutual funds were generally regarded as conservative acquirers of seasoned equities for long-term investment. In 1965, however, institutional investors on the average turned over 21 percent of their portfolios. This indicated rather significantly that many funds had become heavy in-and-out traders in the market, seeking to report to their shareholders sizable capital gains over and above their regular dividend income. Some funds indeed gained a reputation for "performance," and the securities they bought (when that information became available) were carefully noted and frequently bought also by shrewd individual traders. This big-volume buying by funds and active traders was important in carrying certain of the above issues to their highs in 1965. Equally, however, liquidation of certain issues by funds may set in motion a chain of liquidation orders so that institutional action on the selling side can become a powerful actual and psychological market depressant. We can hardly expect to find a stock that is likely to double swiftly among those issues being sold by funds, especially by those with notable records of prior success in market trading. Thus, for guidance in your own speculative decisions about the more actively traded and popular issues, it may be very useful for you to watch "what the funds are doing." They are not always right, but their decisions are made by trained market professionals with their reputations, and sometimes their jobs, depending on their evaluations of securities and trends.

1966 MARKET DOUBLERS

Whereas 1965 was, along with 1961, a classically fine year for market trading, 1966 was a real dud. The NYSE market as a whole dipped 20 percent in the year, and it took a real virtuoso to double between January and December. In fact, we had to stretch a bit to come up with three!

1966 DOUBLERS ON NYSE

STOCK	FIRST SALE OF YEAR	LAST SALE OF YEAR
American Research & Development	20 1/4	40 (almost)
Howmet	20 3/8	48 1/4
Braniff Airways	36 3/8	70 (almost)

Here the explanations are simple. American Research invests in young companies and provides guidance in their development into profitable and successful enterprises. In 1966, one of the companies it had invested in and sponsored, Digital Equipment, made great strides and its stock gained greatly in value. This gain was reflected in ARD.

Howmet (formerly Howe Sound Company) moved up on notable gains in earnings. Braniff reflected excellent advance in earnings and the market leverage created by a rather small floating supply of stock, with about 80 percent of the common held by Greatamerica Corporation.

We can, in fact, glean little from NYSE market action in 1966, except to observe once again that the favorable climate provided by a bull market is most essential if you seek stocks that double in a year. Even companies with earnings advancing spectacularly have a tough time swimming against the tide of a bear market, and 1966 was a bear year!

14

doublers on the american stock exchange in 1965 and 1966

Our avowed goal is swift capital gain; and in our ceaseless quest for this, we are far more interested in potential market velocity than in intrinsic investment quality. From this viewpoint, the approximately 1,050 issues on the American Stock Exchange offer a more fertile hunting ground for speculation than does the Big Board. This is true for several reasons.

SMALLER ISSUES, THINNER MARKETS

American Exchange listings are generally of much smaller companies, often in an early development stage and growing at much faster rates than the corporate giants on the New York Stock Exchange. To illustrate, on February 1, 1966, the average market value per issue of stocks listed on ASE was about $27 million, against an average value per issue on NYSE of roughly $420 million. On the same date, the trading price of the average ASE issue was about $18 a share, against approximately $50 for shares on NYSE. Lower price ranges invariably attract more speculators and generate more extensive and more animated trading activity. However, probably the most important factor responsible for the dazzling trading swings which occur on ASE is small average capitalization. On the Big Board, at least 700,000 outstanding shares held by the public are required for listing. The ASE minimum is only 250,000 shares, and in many issues the floating supply is amazingly thin. In such instances, an order to buy as little as 2,000 shares of a stock selling at $5 can move the market up half a point or more (10 percent). This action, reported in the papers, may attract the attention of speculators and inject heavy buying power into an issue already very thin on the offering side — and the market may start an upward surge aided and abetted by scarcity of offerings. On any average trading day on ASE, you can observe many issues in which the total trading volume does not exceed $5,000. Just a little extra volume — whether buying or selling — can stimulate erratic price swings in such issues.

Because they sell in lower price ranges, stocks on ASE are more prone to double than higher priced shares on the Big Board. A stock selling at 5 is more than twice as likely to double in a given time interval than one at 50. Further, since the average ASE issue has far fewer shares outstanding, aggressive buying can stimulate swift price rises due to relative scarcity of the stock in question.

Other factors conducive to wider percentage swings on the American Stock Exchange are: (1) ASE issues are usually of younger companies, often growing at faster rates than their brethren on NYSE; (2)· trading by individuals accounts for a larger percentage of total volume (over 50 percent) on ASE, accompanied by less institutional buying than on the Big Board. (Institutional buying as a rule is much less speculative in character.)

With this short reference to the more energized and bouncy trading climate on ASE, we present that exchange's Hit Parade for 1965: altogether, 104 stocks that advanced by at least 100 percent in value.

1965 DOUBLERS ON ASE

STOCK	FIRST SALE OF YEAR	LAST SALE OF YEAR
Allegheny Airlines	4 3/8	13
Allied Control	7 1/8	24 5/8
Alloys Unlimited	13 1/8	46
American Beverage	3 1/2	9 3/8
American Book Company	10 7/8	23 7/8
American Electronics	1	2 3/8
American Safety Equipment	5 1/4	13
Andrea Radio	7 5/8	24
Argus, Inc.	3 1/4	8 3/4
Asamera Oil	5/8	2 1/2
Astrex	2 1/4	6 3/8
Audio Devices	8 1/8	22 5/8
Automatic Radio	2 1/8	4 5/8
Avien	1/2	3 1/2
Banff Oil	1 1/8	7 1/4
Bell Electronics	1 7/8	5
Berkey Photo (Moved to NYSE during year)	19 3/8	39 1/8
Bowling Corporation of America	1 3/8	2 3/4
Bowser	5 1/2	12
Caldor	10 1/4	23 1/2
CCI	1 1/2	3 5/8
Century Geophysical	2 5/8	10 3/4
Chief Consolidated Mining	2 5/8	5 5/8
Chromalloy American	15 5/8	35 5/8
Clarostat Manufacturing	5 5/8	11 3/8
Computer Sciences	7 3/4	21 5/8
Condec	4 7/8	10 1/4
Continental Aviation	8	16 1/2
Cubic	4 7/8	10 3/4
Dixilyn	2 1/2	9 1/8
Duraloy	2 1/8	6 3/8

STOCK	FIRST SALE OF YEAR	LAST SALE OF YEAR
Dynalectron	3	6 5/8
Eastern Air Devices	3/4	6 3/4
Eckerd Drugs (Florida)	12 1/2	26
Elco	10 1/4	23
Electro-Voice	5 1/2	17 1/8
Electronic Communications	8 1/2	17 7/8
Espey Manufacturing & Electronics	4	9 7/8
M. H. Fishman	10 1/8	24 7/8
Flying Tiger Line	9 1/2	28 1/4
Frontier Airlines	8 1/8	18 5/8
General Alloys	2 5/8	6
A. C. Gilbert	9 1/4	20 3/8
Gordon Jewelry	13 1/2	34 1/4
GTI	3 1/8	9 1/4
Gulf American	4 7/8	10 1/4
H & B American	3 3/8	6 3/4
C. M. Hall Lamp	2 3/4	11 1/2
R. Hoe	3	6 7/8
Philip A. Hunt Chemical	12 3/4	29 1/8
Hycon	6 3/4	15 7/8
IMC Magnetics	3 1/8	6 3/8
Jefferson Lake Petro-chemicals	9 1/16	22 1/2
Walter Kidde	16	45 3/4
Lee Motor Products	1 1/4	2 1/2
Lockwood, Kessler & Bartlett	2 1/8	8 3/4
Lundy Electronics & Systems	6 1/4	16 3/4
Mallory Randall	1 3/4	5
Maul Brothers	4 1/4	11 1/4
Microwave Associates	9 5/8	21 1/2
Mohawk Airlines	6 1/4	16 3/4
Monogram Industries	7	15 7/8

STOCK	FIRST SALE OF YEAR	LAST SALE OF YEAR
Morse Electro Products	1	2 3/8
National Video	8 3/8	83 1/2
Northeast Airlines	4 1/2	31 5/8
Pacific Northern Airlines	3 3/4	14 1/2
Pioneer Aerodynamic Systems	3	10 1/8
Planning Research	12	34
Pneumo Dynamics	16 7/8	42 1/4
Poloron Products	2 1/4	6
Potter Instrument	6 3/4	16
Robinson Technical Products	3 3/4	8 3/8
Rodney Metals	4 1/2	9
Rowland Products	8 3/4	34 1/4
Royal American Industries	11/16	1 1/2
Ryan Consolidated Petroleum	2 7/8	6 3/8
Seaboard World Airlines	6	14
Sealectro	4 3/8	9 1/4
Seeman Brothers	4 1/8	9
Sel-Rex	11 5/8	24 3/4
Simmonds Precision Products	7 3/4	56 1/2
Slick	5 1/4	11 1/2
Solitron Devices	39 1/2	132 1/4
Soss Manufacturing	9 1/4	19 3/8
Southern Realty & Utilities	1	3 1/2
Speed-O-Print Business Machines	7 1/8	15 7/8
Stanley Aviation	4	10 3/4
Statham Instruments	14 5/8	29 3/8
Sunair Electronics	2	4 3/8
Supronics	1 1/8	2 3/4
Syntex	32 7/8	97 7/8
Technical Operations	19 1/2	47 1/4
Teleprompter	6 7/8	19 1/4

STOCK	LAST SALE OF YEAR	FIRST SALE OF YEAR
Television Industries	5/8	2
Tenney Engineering	1 3/4	4
Terminal-Hudson Electronics	2 1/4	6
Thompson-Starrett	1 1/4	5 7/8
Universal Automated Industries	9/16	3 1/2
Weiman	5 3/4	15 5/8
Western Equities	7 5/8	42 7/8
Western Nuclear	5 1/4	14
Wieboldt Stores	6 5/8	17
Williamhouse	7 5/8	15 1/2
XTRA	9 1/8	51

Here indeed is excellent proof that we are on the right track. There are plenty of stocks that can double in a year. Almost one stock out of every ten on ASE *doubled in 1965*; and a number of these recorded far greater gains. Altogether, twelve of the above advanced between 200 and 300 percent; five advanced 300 to 400 percent; two 400 to 500 percent; and five stocks (Avien, Eastern Air Devices, National Video, Northeast Airlines, and Simmonds Precision Products) delighted their holders by gaining over 500 percent! The champ was National Video, which grew by almost 900 percent.

WHAT PUSHED THEM UP?

It would be nice to think that all these gains were logical and impelled by such fundamental forces as dramatic improvement in earnings or rising dividend payments; but these propulsive forces are notably absent. Take Avien, a little aircraft-supply company making no money but rather suspended in that twilight zone of solvency, Chapter XI of the Bankruptcy Act (I've never learned what the other ten chapters covered). New capital was located for this troubled company, and Avien shares responded by leaping from 50 cents to $3.50; and 70 percent of Avien capitalization of 1,370,000 shares turned over during the year.

Northeast Airlines is another trader's darling that made the grade without benefit of earnings. The company had been losing money for several years but got a new lease on life when it was granted a license to run from Boston and New York to Miami. The other lines weren't exactly crazy about this, and attempts were made to eliminate Northeast from this lucrative run. But the license was retained; some new planes were added; and, most important, in 1965 Storer Broadcasting Company gained control by buying a block of Northeast at around $5 a share. That's all that was needed. In the most favorable market climate for airlines since 1946, Northeast took off with a tailwind, gaining 600 percent altitude for the year. Other airline issues sparkling on ASE in 1965 included Allegheny, Continental Aviation, Flying Tiger, Frontier, Mohawk, Pacific Northern, and Seaboard World. It was a great year to be airborne in the market!

Banff Oil shows what can happen when the drill bit hits the right oilfield. Banff was just an ordinary little "penny" Canadian company, a small producer, when early in 1965 it made a rich crude discovery at (appropriately named) Rainbow Lake in northwest Alberta. Banff was the operator on a sizable chunk of oil-prone terrain — over 46,000 lease acres. Banff had some strong partners, too — Aquitaine Company, owned by the huge French government oil complex, and Mobil Oil. Out of the first ten wells drilled, six were successful, and an oilfield with reserves of possibly 600 million barrels was indicated. On the strength of this strike, a 240-mile, 20-inch pipeline was immediately planned to run from Rainbow to Nisipi.

While Banff's interest in Rainbow Lake is only 5 percent (Aquitaine has 45 percent and Mobil 50 percent), Banff also has a royalty interest in a gas field at Gold Lake worth around $10 million at the 1965 year end. With all this, Banff earned only 1 cent a share in 1964, before the fireworks began. The stock gained 500 percent in 1965, and doubled again in 1966. Trading for 1965 was about 4 million shares — almost a 100 percent turnover of its 4,215,000 outstanding shares. Banff, listed on both ASE and Toronto, has been a lively performer and appears to have a lot of speculative oomph still left even after its dazzling series of rises.

Accompanying Banff on the Hit Parade of oils were: Asamera, Jefferson Lake, and Ryan Consolidated.

COLOR TV

One of the magic market phrases in 1965 was "color TV." If a company was in or entering this field, it automatically qualified as an "in" stock. The Tiffany of the business, Corning Glass, which makes 75 percent of the color bulbs and whose stock sells majestically in the 300's. was notably ignored. But as we saw on the NYSE, Admiral and Motorola gained roaringly, and color-TV shares were even more fashionable and animate on ASE. National Video showed the way.

National Video, in 1965, was the fourth largest color-TV-tube manufacturer (after RCA, Zenith, and Sylvania). It had had no impressive track record. The stock sold at 3 in 1963 and closed at 8 3/8 in 1964. It earned but 10 cents a share in fiscal 1965 (year ending May 31). Then its sales began to pick up, trebling to an annual rate of around $75 million; profits improved ($1.14 for the half year ending November 30, 1965); and the stock gained an irrepressible following, closing the year at 83 1/2, with lots of drive left over for 1966. Just how a stock so specialized and so dependent on a single competitive product deserved to gain such market altitude is a little hard to see. Others — Motorola, Sylvania, and Admiral — expanded their color-tube production in 1965. Did National Video really justify a market valuation of over $200 at the 1965 year end? Earnings were rising — but that much? Despite these queries, the stock won an enthusiastic following and gained fabulously, which is all we can ask of any stock. At least temporarily.

At the tail of the color-TV-market comet were

a couple of other ASE swingers, Thompson-Starrett and Noramco. Thompson-Starrett not only doubled, but actually gained 370 percent for the year. Its full range was between 1 and 9 1/4. T-S is in reality a building-construction firm with a subsidiary making TV and radio sets. Rumor had it that T-S had come upon a notable technical advance in color TV and the stock shot up like a Titan rocket. As it turned out, the stock earned only 10 cents a share for calendar 1965, and the TV virtuosity was greatly overplayed. Here again the reasons for such a rise were mostly psychological and had little reference to earning power.

Honorable mention is probably due Noramco, which doubled during the year even though it couldn't hold its gains. Noramco's main business is the Dugan Bakery division, a door-to-door bakery company; but a Wall Street rumor had it that the company had the patent rights to a revolutionary new flat color-TV tube. The sheep flocked in and bought Noramco heavily against a total 1.5-million-share capitalization; and the stock zoomed from 3 to 10 within thirty days. It swiftly "fell out of bed," however, after the SEC suspended trading in the issue. The color-TV "breakthrough" was apparently pretty nebulous. In due course, after all that market hoopla, Noramco showed a loss in 1965 — as it had for several earlier years. Another illustration of market gains synthetically induced. (In 1966, Noramco was in Chapter XI of the Bankruptcy Act.)

Further documenting the fact that market leaders in 1965 were heavily concentrated in a few industries, note the roster of electronic performers above: Audio Devices, Automatic Radio, Bell Electronics, Dynalectron, Electronic Communications, Hycon, IMC Magnetics, Lundy Electronics, Microwave Associates, Potter Instrument, Solitron (the most magnificent), Sunair Electronics, Supronics, Television Industries, Terminal-Hudson, and XTRA. In general summary, it is worth noting that in 1965, fifty stocks of those doubling on ASE *started their moves below $5 a share!* This powerfully emphasizes what we mentioned earlier in this chapter: that shares in the $5 zone (or below) are the best ones to look at to find happiness in stocks that double. The greater the risk, the greater the possible reward.

1966 DOUBLERS

Having reviewed a year — 1965 — in which speculation for fun and profit was rampant, we come next to the sobering-up period. In 1966, the DJIA declined 19.8 percent for the year and ASE got the message and declined in similar manner. On the American Stock Exchange, the doublers were as follows:

1966 DOUBLERS ON ASE

STOCK	FIRST SALE OF YEAR	LAST SALE OF YEAR
Arwood	8 3/4	18 7/8
Atco Chemical-Industrial Products	2 1/4	5
Banff Oil	7 3/16	15 1/2
Canaveral International	1 7/8	4
Dome Petroleum	14 1/2	33 3/8
Esquire	23 1/2	67 3/4
R. Hoe	6 7/8	30
Jefferson Construction	3 5/8	7 7/8
Monogram Industries	7 7/8	15 5/8 (almost)
Rodney Metals	8 3/4	18 5/8
Saxon Paper	7 7/8	15 5/8 (almost)
Stanrock Uranium Mines	3/4	1 3/4
Talley Industries	9 5/8	19 5/8

Only thirteen stocks of the more than one thousand listed managed to double. Of these, two reflected the big Canadian oil strike at Rainbow Lake (Banff and Dome). Esquire responded to a powerful advance in net earnings; Jefferson Construction got a merger invitation; Stanrock was sensitive to the brighter long-term outlook for uranium. Nearly every one, on inspection, will be found to have a rather small capitalization and thus able to reflect sensitively favorable corporate developments. The main message we can get from these performers is again that it helps to start out low. *All but two* started their rise from below $10 a share!

This chapter concludes our six-year review of listed stocks that have doubled. It covers an interesting group of securities and provides the background for analysis, given in the next chapter, of the dominant and often distinguishing attributes of performance stocks. These qualities or characteristics are, in fact, seldom evident in conservative dividend-paying stocks of large, mature companies. If you seek stocks that double in a year, you often find them in the byways — not the highways!

15

characteristics of stocks that double in a year

We have, in the preceding chapters, presented lists of those stocks on the New York and American Stock Exchanges that have doubled in the calendar years 1961-66. By analyzing the performances of these individual issues, we are now able to draw some general conclusions about the qualities and characteristics that distinguish this group of equities from their less animate market brethren. Our theory from the outset has been that stocks possessing many of the attributes of these winners are much more likely to post dramatic market gains — and even to double — in 1967 than speculative issues chosen at random or merely on the basis of indicated increases in per-share earnings. Accordingly, and without further prelude, we present below the more dominant and recurrent characteristics of companies whose shares have doubled in past years.

1. Many are located in dynamically growing industries, such as electronics and savings-and-loan companies in 1961; airlines in 1963; minerals in 1964; TV, airlines, publishing, and business-machines in 1965.

2. Many are aggressively and successfully merger-minded (U. S. Industries, Ward Foods, Occidental Petroleum, Gulf & Western Industries, Royal American, Walter Kidde, Ling-Temco-Vought, Litton).

3. Their stocks sell at an average price below $25 a share if on NYSE: and below $10 if on ASE at the time they start their 100 percent climbs.

4. They are aggressively, and imaginatively, managed, usually by younger men — below fifty.

5. Their stocks are in most cases substantially held (from 10 percent to a majority of outstanding common) by men dominant in management and animated by zeal for capital gains.

6. Many frequently have relatively small capitalizations, substantially leveraged by senior securities (Chicago & North Western, Boston & Maine, Greatamerica).

7. Substantial amounts of their shares are closely held, leaving a small floating supply. Enthusiastic buying of a stock with small floating supply can create dynamic price swings (Valley Metallurgical Processing, Solitron Devices, Polaroid, Chicago & North Western, Alloys Unlimited, in 1965-66).

8. They scintillate because of new mineral strikes or technological breakthroughs (Texas Gulf Sulphur, Banff Oil, Dome Petroleum, Bunker Hill, Syntex, Cinerama, Xerox, Polaroid, SCM, Dymo Industries).

9. They benefit from strong sponsorship created by market letters or recommendations by one or several leading brokerage houses or investment services. The buying power generated by a single major firm with many branches is often enough to jet-propel a popular stock to exciting new highs.

10. When growth companies move from market obscurity to a point where institutions begin buying their shares, a powerful price uptrend usually ensues. This was a feature of airline performance beginning in 1961 and in S&L shares in the same year.

11. When company shares move to listed status, they often pick up market momentum. This is due to publicity created by daily reporting of trading activity and volume. Occidental Petroleum, Braniff Airways, Consolidated Freightways, CTS, Holiday Inns, and Comsat, all moved forward briskly after being listed on NYSE.

12. The newer romantic industries always

seem to generate far greater market action than old standbys, such as cement, construction, food products, utilities, trucking, textiles, steels. For some reason, traders accord very high multiples to growth stocks in newer fields: scientific-electronic instrumentation, business machines, optics, and the like. Comsat was a hot stock before it earned a dime, and Solitron, Xerox, and IBM consistently sell at gaudy P/E multiples. Certain it is that buying a stock just because its P/E ratio is low offers no assurance that it will go up; and dazzling prospects are far more persuasive to price advances than dividend payments or expectations.

13. Company shares increasing in net earnings by 30 percent or more a year are likely to double.

14. Special situations are laws unto themselves, but can be most rewarding if properly analyzed and appraised. Ward Foods in 1961 and Brazilian Traction in 1964 were both special and rewarding situations. (Brown Company and Carter-Wallace may prove interesting special situations in 1967.) Where company shares have been notably depressed (as cements, S&L's, and life-insurance stocks in 1966), they often present excellent rebound opportunities for doubling in a later year.

15. Stocks with inherent capability of doubling are, of course, far more likely to do so in surging bull markets, as in 1961 and 1965, than in dull or declining markets, as in 1962 and 1966. Further, doublers in a year are seldom found among the two hundred largest companies (ex-

ceptions: W. R. Grace, Crown Cork & Seal, National Cash Register in 1965).

In conclusion, the most dynamic of these forces for market upsurge are (1) earnings increasing 50 percent or more in a year, (2) small stock capitalization and floating supply, (3) a fashionable industry, (4) strong sponsorship, (5) low price — below $25 on NYSE and below $10 on ASE, and (6) leverage. There are few year-after-year repeaters among stocks that double in a twelve-month period.

Review the above list of attributes when searching for hot stocks. They offer you no absolute assurance of success or gain, but they should place you in a profit-prone terrain.

Our next chapters will be the most daring ones in the entire book. Armed with all the ammunition stored in the earlier chapters, we shall endeavor, with judgment tempered by knowledge of the performance characteristics of past winners, to nominate a group of stocks with a chance to double in 1967. This is obviously a rash endeavor since, as you have seen, in some years doubling is virtually impossible. We shall need a very bullish year to push a respectable percentage of these candidates into the winners' circle. Even in roaring markets, most of the old-pro traders are content to record a 50 percent gain over a two-year stretch.

This book started out intrepid, however, and it's too late to turn mousy now. So brace yourself for the last chapters, and for a unique list of hopeful equities that, by their performance, will either call for a sequel to this book a year hence, or dispatch its author to a long hitch in the Foreign Legion. Happiness is a stock that doubles — or else!

16

selection of possible doublers in 1967: life insurance stocks

Now we're coming into the home stretch of the book and to its most exciting part. We're ready to put to work the knowledge we gained earlier about such trading guidelines as fundamentals, charts, leverage, P/E ratios, growth stocks, special situations, and so on; and to blend this wisdom with a perception of some of the dominant characteristics of listed stocks that have doubled since 1960.

Before unveiling the 1967 list, however, we

must define our ground rules. For our purposes all of the stocks listed earlier that doubled were those that sold on the last trading day in December at prices 100 percent or more above their opening prices for that year. We had to set certain time limits; and to follow the book title faithfully, we have reported doublers in this manner. (Many additional stocks in each year gained 100 percent or more from their lows to their highs.)

In selecting possible doublers for 1967, we were faced with an obvious book production problem. All the stocks screened for possible stellar performance in 1967 were selected and researched prior to December 31, 1966, and our first thought was to offer this list as of January 1, 1967. This required some editorial consideration, however, because while these issues were in our typewriter within a few weeks after December 31, 1966, they could not possibly appear in the published book until some four or five months later in the year. (This is how long it takes to produce a hard-cover book.) Most stocks offered by brokers for your consideration are, as you know, given on an up-to-the-minute basis with latest quotations, whereas we were faced with at least a 120-day time lag. Many readers would be sure to say that if certain selections we made moved briskly by publication time, we'd picked them after they had already advanced. Well, we didn't! These were all December 31 babies. But we did make one compromise. We felt that 1967 might be a reasonably strong market year, rebounding from the 737 DJIA low of 1966 to perhaps 925. We felt, however, that if President Johnson announced a 15 percent tax rise (which seemed possible at the time), market psychology would be gloomy for months thereafter, and hopes of a climate favorable to the doubling of specially screened stocks would be dashed. Had a tax increase of 15 percent been presented by the President, we would have called off publication due to wet grounds!

Accordingly, we admit we hedged a little. We waited until the President delivered his State of the Union message on January 10, and when all he asked for was a 6 percent surtax, we felt that 1967 had a valid chance to be a bull year and that stocks selected might perform creditably. So we priced every stock we had screened, as of the market close of January 11, 1967, the day after the President's speech, and that's the starting date in our book. The terminal date is December 30, 1967. The stocks described in the pages that follow are supposed to double in this interval. We hope and believe that some of them will. A guy is great in baseball if he bats .300. We'd settle for that. For the market to perform thus, however, the Vietnam War must get no angrier, interest rates must continue to moderate, building construction must improve, the British pound must stay solvent, labor demands must be reasonable, the OTC market must become more popular, and many tired stocks, such as cements, life insurance, and S&L's, must return to some measure of popularity. We don't ask a lot — just a few essential trappings of a buoyant market climate.

THE INDUSTRIAL APPROACH

We're dividing into two groups our catalog of stocks that may have something better than a Chinaman's chance of doubling: (1) stocks in certain favorably placed industries, and (2) diversified selections or special situations.

Of the industries that appear attractively positioned to do better in 1967, we have selected three: life insurance, oil, and savings and loan. We'll take up life insurance first.

LIFE-INSURANCE STOCKS

Life insurance is one of the fastest growing major industries in America, with $166 billion in assets and $1 trillion of life insurance in force. There's not a single stock issue of any operating life-insurance company listed on any exchange. Of the approximately 1,640 life-insurance companies, some 1,500 of them are stock companies, doing about 42 percent of the business, with the lion's share (58 percent) done by mutual companies (owned by policyholders). Some of these mutuals are huge, such as Metropolitan, Prudential, Equitable, Mutual of New York, John Hancock.

Some of the most dramatic capital gains have been recorded over the years in life stocks.

Between 1954 and 1964, shares in the ten largest stock life-insurance companies gained on the average over 600 percent in price!

DOLDRUMS, 1964-66

The life-stock market, however, went into the doldrums in April, 1964, from which it did not begin to emerge until late October, 1966. Why was this? (1) Because life stocks were probably selling too high in 1964 (30 times adjusted earnings) and discounting growth too far ahead; (2) because the whole stock market declined by 20 percent in 1966; (3) because investors and speculators showed strong preference for performance, or action, stocks—Polaroid, Fairchild, Syntex, etc.—which trade in great daily volume and often with dramatic price swings; (4) because of the fashion of buying stocks selected by technical (chart-type) analysis rather than by fundamentals; and (5) because of a spate of new life-company share offerings in 1964 and 1965, which tended to glut the market.

In any event, many fine life stocks sold off sharply during this period—some by as much as 40 or 45 percent. As a result, it appears that seasoned life issues look underpriced and gainful as 1967 opens, particularly in view of their substantial year-by-year gains in assets, earnings, and insurance in force. To document this financial forward motion, we suggest that you note the gains recorded by the entire industry in one year—1966.

LIFE-INSURANCE INDUSTRY

	ESTIMATED 1966	ACTUAL 1965
Life insurance in force	$980 billion	$900 billion
Total premium income (life, annuity, and accident & health)	$26.5 billion	$24.6 billion
Total investment income	$7.3 billion	$6.75 billion
Total assets	$166.8 billion	$158.8 billion
Sales for year	$121.5 billion	$114.32 billion
Total outstanding policies	330 million	320.1 million
Average family-owned insurance	$15,800	$14,700
Earned on investments	4.71 percent	4.61 percent

This attractive across-the-board growth in 1966 is no isolated phenomenon, but continues an amazing uptrend extending without hiatus since 1933. Where life stocks sold at 30 times adjusted earnings in March, 1964, they now sell at around 17 or 18 times; and yet earnings of seasoned companies have advanced notably in the interim. Other plus factors are: (1) the rising percentage of the population in the twenty-five-year age group (the largest market for life insurance), and (2) the investment opportunities of life companies, the most attractive in forty years. (For twenty years, the return on life-insurance investments has advanced without pause, from 2.88 percent in 1947 to 4.71 percent in 1966.) Investment of new money in 1967 should return more than 6 percent before taxes. Mortality experience has improved slightly and might advance dramatically if we suddenly found cures for heart disease and cancer. Automation is holding down the costs of life-insurance-company operation and, in any event, operating costs of life companies average below 18 percent of total income. There is no labor problem here; no inventory loss; no changing annual fashions or models.

LEVERAGE

Not well enough understood is the leverage of stock life-insurance companies. They guarantee to pay their insured, on the average, around a 3 percent return on policy reserves invested. Thus, with investment averaging 4.71 percent in 1966 (before taxes), an income of 1.71 percent on invested reserves for the year is indicated for the representative company. To be specific, if a stock company had $100 million in invested reserves in 1966, the portion of pretax income flowing to stockholders would have been $1,710,000, or $1.71 a share if there were 1 million capital shares outstanding. This leverage, created by the margin between tabular interest and actual interest earned, is a powerful factor in life-company earnings. And the compounding of these interest overages occurs year after year.

Another point to note is that life-insurance companies seldom pay out more than 20 percent of net gain from operation; so that substantial retained earnings, not distributed or taxable to shareholders, compound year after year to rapidly enhance book values.

From the foregoing, there appears a solid basis for belief that life stocks may prove resurgent, and that some may even double in 1967. They benefit from earnings growing 8 percent annually, and from a market depressed excessively in the past two years.

Our selections for possible 100 percent gain in 1967 would be:

1. Life Insurance Company of Kentucky
2. Liberty Life Insurance Company
3. National Investors Life Insurance Company

LIFE INSURANCE COMPANY OF KENTUCKY

This is an energetic life-insurance company not ten years old, yet with some $670 million of life insurance in force. At the end of 1960, it had only $74.3 million of insurance in force, assets of only $4 million, and an adjusted net worth per share of $1.84. At the 1966 year end, estimated figures were: assets $30 million, adjusted net worth per share $11, and net gain from operations $925,000 (against only $313,000 in 1965).

This outstanding growth rate gives evidence of an energetic, progressive management and suggests that Life of Kentucky capital stock may be substantially undervalued at its January 11, 1967, quotation of 20 7/8. Adjusted earnings per share were $1.85 in 1965, around $2 for 1966, and may reach $2.50 in 1967. Selling at around

10 times earnings, Life of Kentucky appears to be priced at a multiple considerably below other comparable life equities.

Kentucky Life has an aggressive sales program, an ultramodern line of contracts, including a new college-education policy. In the first six months of 1966, it increased total income by 18.5 percent, and its investment income by 34 percent. The company should be making new investments in 1967 at rates of better than 6 percent.

In conclusion, we feel that Life Insurance Company of Kentucky stock, outstanding in the amount of 1,564,870 shares, has the earning power and dynamics to sell in the 40's in 1967, or double its present quotation.

LIBERTY LIFE INSURANCE COMPANY

This is the largest life-insurance company in South Carolina, and the forty-first largest stock company in the nation. It is licensed to do business in twenty-one states, the District of Columbia, and Puerto Rico, and has over $2 billion of life insurance in force. It is a sixty-year-old company of real substance, with total assets above $200 million.

A feature of Liberty Life is its sales aggressiveness, with over one thousand full-time agents and some thirty-six general agents, offering a portfolio including all the standard insurance, accident, and health contracts. Liberty writes substantial amounts of group credit life insurance and individual borrower's insurance on the lives of mortgagors through contracts with about 620 savings-and-loan associations. This is attractive business flowing regularly to the company without individual solicitation. Liberty has also developed its ACC-U-COMP system, a computerized method of defining the insurance needs of each applicant, which usually leads to higher unit sales than traditional selling methods.

Corporate operating efficiency is at a high level due to installation, in 1966, of a big IBM 360 computer, which can handle policy calculations, billing, and investment data.

Liberty Life has been steadily increasing annual earnings on its 4,125,000 shares of capital stock (36.5 percent closely held). Adjusted per share net was about $1.38 in 1965 and probably over $1.60 in 1966. Book value is approximately $8.50. Liberty Life should grow at an annual rate of 10 percent or better, and the stock at 20 3/4 should this year cross its 1965 high of 33. A solid company, apparently undervalued.

NATIONAL INVESTORS LIFE INSURANCE COMPANY (LITTLE ROCK, ARKANSAS)

Here is an unusual company. Organized only ten years ago, it now (12/31/66) has $456,278,117 of insurance in force and is licensed to do business in Arkansas, Louisiana, Mississippi, and Oklahoma. It writes all the standard forms of life insurance and annuities.

Not only is National Investors Life a significant company in its own right, but it is shepherd to a substantial semiaffiliated group of growing life companies in many states, also founded by Mr. Jess Odom (President of NILIC) and associates. For these companies NILIC handles reinsurance (above individual retention levels) and, under service agreements, performs underwriting functions, prepares policies for insurance suppliers, maintains policyholder records and files, prepares production reports, premium notices, commission statements, and annual reports. Much of this servicing work is done by an IBM 360 computer and extensive data-processing equipment in NILIC's home-office building in Little Rock.

For these services, NILIC charges 12.5 percent of the first-year premium (received by the contracting company) and 3 percent of annual premiums thereafter. This arrangement creates an almost annuity-type (and expanding) income flow to NILIC, in addition to its own direct earnings from operation. (Income from these services was $410,000 in 1966.)

Because of the aggressive management of NILIC and its rapid growth from $65 million of insurance in force in 1961 to $456,278,117 at the 1966 year end, we see much speculative merit in National Investors Life capital stock (1,049,352 shares outstanding) at 7 3/4. Much of this stock is closely held, and NILIC has unusual leverage for growth due to its service contracts with companies (some quite closely affiliated). NILIC might develop enough momentum to cross 16 in 1967.

17

possible doublers: oil-production speculations

The oil industry seldom looked better than at the 1966 year end. Petroleum supplies roughly 55 percent of the world's energy. The demand for petroleum products is rising about 9 percent annually in Europe and 5 percent in the United States. The big problem is to find enough oil to keep up with these huge and insistent global demands. Possibly the two hottest fields for oil exploration and potential future production are (1) offshore areas, near such places as Louisiana, Libya, Nigeria, Saudi Arabia, and Borneo, and in the North Sea, and (2) Rainbow Lake in Alberta. These oil-prone swaths of geography provide, we believe, some notable opportunities for successful speculation.

OFFSHORE

Offshore drilling from underwater fields off twenty countries now supplies about 15 percent of the free world's oil. Undersea drilling is very expensive, however, because rigs cost a lot and drilling goes much deeper than onshore. Most important offshore drilling is financed by the big international companies, whose shares are not very likely to double in a year. The drilling itself, however, is very largely done by smaller independent drilling contractors; and it is among these companies that we observe unusual potentials for swift market gains derived indirectly from oil production. There are four standard kinds of offshore drilling rigs: (1) submersible barges that sit on the bottom; (2) self-elevating platforms set on adjustable legs, which can drill in various depths up to 300 feet; (3) surface drilling vessels operating in water up to 600 feet deep; and (4) semisubmersible craft, which can operate either on the bottom or at selected depths, or be towed to other drill sites. The most expensive barges can cost as much as $10 million per unit.

SANTA FE DRILLING COMPANY

Probably the most substantial company in the business is J. Ray McDermott & Company, but its stock is too high to double easily. Our preference would be Santa Fe Drilling Company, with a compact capitalization of 1,626,000 shares listed on NYSE and selling on January 11, 1967, at 29 1/8.

Santa Fe is a leading international drilling contractor, which grossed around $37 million in 1966 and earned around $1.90. For 1967, we expect gross to jump to $44 million and a per share net of close to $2.50. Heavy-equipment depreciation generates a cash flow that should exceed $11 million ($7 a share) in 1967. The company, as of November 1, 1966, owns and operates fifty-one drilling rigs, drilling on- and offshore in twelve countries, and operates twelve rigs for others. Marine drillers are usually paid on a daily rental basis, which will average around $8,000 a day for a $6 million rig.

Santa Fe in the past did most of its drilling on land but anticipates getting 50 percent of revenues from offshore by 1970. It is expected by then that total annual gross may reach $70 million.

Santa Fe Drilling should enjoy maximum demand for its expanding drilling units for some years to come. Its stock benefits from a strong earnings upthrust and from the leverage created by $20 million in debt. The stock should attract an eager trading following in 1967, moving the issue possibly to the 55 zone.

GLOBAL MARINE

Our second drilling candidate is Global Marine, Inc., with 1,812,467 shares of common outstanding, preceded by $22.6 million in debt and 68,000 shares of $5 convertible preferred (the senior securities creating powerful leverage for the common). Global Marine is a specialist in ship-shaped floating drilling vessels, quite mobile, with the largest able to drill in 600 feet of water. These vessels are in great demand for the deeper drilling now in vogue, and have had a notable record for safety and reliability.

The company is strongly sponsored, with J. H. Whitney & Company and J. H. Hillman & Sons, plus officers and directors believed to own altogether about 50 percent of the common. Revenues of around $30 million for 1966 might grow to $36 million plus in 1967; and per share net may expand from an indicated $1.80 in 1966 to at least $2.20 in 1967. Four new heavy-drilling units, costing $7 million each, are to be constructed in 1967, with one now under way and expected to go into operation probably by August.

Global Marine common trades OTC and could turn in a steller performance this year. Quotation on January 11, 1967, was 30 1/2.

Both Santa Fe and Global have the makings of action stocks — all they need is a following that exalts their price/earnings multiple adequately. Two alternate offshore entries would be Zapata Off-Shore, which has already advanced smartly, and Reading & Bates Offshore Drilling, a highly leveraged common at about $13.

ALBERTA OIL SHARES

While we discussed the gleaning of money from oil indirectly by supplying the greatly needed drilling barges at rewarding rentals, we propose now to go after the oil direct, and in a special "hot" area — northwest Alberta. Here, in February of 1965, Banff Oil (in association with Aquitaine and Mobil) brought in a discovery well at Rainbow Lake that flowed 3,600 barrels a day. Extensive further drilling in the area by Banff and others brought in twenty-seven wells adjacent to Rainbow Lake; and the field is averaging better than 17,000 barrels per day. In the whole area, fifty wells have become productive of oil, gas, or both.

Competent oil geologists now view the Rainbow-Zama Lake region as drawing on a deep Middle Devonian formation, extending northwest over 1,000 miles from North Dakota to British Columbia; and containing fields that may expand Canada's oil reserves from 8.2 billion barrels (current estimate) to over 15 billion barrels by 1970. In any event, the region is hot, with land prices of $7,500 to $10,000 an acre being paid for acreage not too remote from existing wells at Rainbow Lake.

Obviously the best positioned companies are those that acquired extensive land holdings in the area earlier. They can drill, or sell their acreage out at a big profit. Banff stock rose from a 1965 low of 1 1/8 to a 1966 high of 18 1/4; and other selected issues here hopefully may perform rewardingly.

CANADIAN SUPERIOR OIL, LTD.

Our first choice in west Canada is Canadian Superior Oil, Ltd. The 8,501,506 shares (53.6 percent owned by the Superior Oil Company) are listed on both the Toronto and American Stock Exchanges, with the January 11, 1967, quotation 29 7/8 in New York. Here is a company with fine management, producing 7,534,474 barrels of oil and concentrate in 1965, about 72 percent from Alberta fields. Net income was 55 cents a share in 1965, but this understates the picture, since the company charges off exploration and development in the year incurred. Net for 1966 was about 70 cents.

Land holdings are most extensive, with net acreage holdings of 7,206,760 in Canada alone, plus some 7,300,000 acres in foreign holdings. Of its Dominion holdings, Canadian Superior owns interests varying from 33.5 to 100 percent in over 500,000 acres in the Rainbow-Zama and Steen River and Bistcho River areas. Substantial new production brought in from only a small part of this wide area could affect share quotations dramatically.

Canadian Superior common appears to be an excellent vehicle for speculation in Alberta oil, with a significant stake in Rainbow Lake. Its common is selected for doubling in 1967.

PROVO GAS PRODUCERS, LTD.

Provo is not particularly well known to American investors. The company has expanded in the past five years from basic natural-gas production into oil and LPG production and marketing. Within the past year, however, it has attracted market attention because of its undeveloped lease and permit acreage totaling 1,567,337 net acres as of June 30, 1966. This acreage is in the Steen River region of Alberta, some forty miles northwest of Rainbow Lake, and thirty miles south of recent Provo and Dome gas discoveries in the Bistcho Lake region. Apart from this strategically situated land, Provo earned $704,000 net in the first half of 1966 on its 8,741,916 common shares (38 percent held by Dome Petroleum). Gross for the full year should reach $8 million, with 45 cents a share in cash flow. There are also 180,000 warrants outstanding to buy common at $3.50 currently. Current quote (January 11, 1967) is $5.30 on the Toronto Stock Exchange. With a little bit of luck, the stock might reacn 12 in 1967.

CENTRAL-DEL RIO OILS, LTD.

This is a lively company with plenty of working capital — $4.9 million net at June 30, 1966. Its land holding, as of December 31, 1965, amounted to 4,337,925 gross acres. Through Central Leduc Oils, a wholly owned subsidiary, the company has properties in North Dakota, Montana, Louisiana, and New Mexico.

Central-Del Rio is not sitting around waiting for land values to go up, but is active in the exploration and development of oil and gas lands in Saskatchewan, Alberta, and British Columbia. In 1965, the company sold 3,370,000 barrels and earned 50 cents a share on its 6,580,324 shares of common stock. It is widely believed that Central-Del Rio has a portion of its holdings well positioned in relation to the Rainbow Lake strike.

Central-Del Rio could "catch on" rapidly if it made a new strike on its properties. Meanwhile, the issue looks as if it is under steady accumulation. We think it has a chance to double in 1967 from the early January price of 13 1/4.

CANADIAN EXPORT GAS & OIL

This is a lesser company and a small producer, but its prospects benefit from its holdings of 1.5 million acres (gross) northeast of Rainbow Lake and presumably well within the "Keg River Trend." No notable wells have yet been driven on these lands, but farmed-out exploration agreements have been made with majors, such as Mobil, Imperial, and Cities, with retained interests varying between 25 and 50 percent. Of 7.8 million shares outstanding (listed in Toronto and on ASE), Newmont Mining Company owns 20 percent. Here you speculate not on earning power (only 15 cents a share in 1966) but on the hope of a significant strike with the drill bit. This stock can stay where it is or sell past $10 in 1967. We take the more optimistic view!

18

possible doublers: savings-and-loan shares

The savings-and-loan industry is a huge one, having $133 billion in assets and functioning as the major supplier of mortgage money to the home owners of America. Over 90 percent of savings-and-loan associations across America are mutual (owned in theory by their account holders), and the balance (about six-hundred) are institutions with publicly held stock (like commercial banks). The largest of these stock companies are in California, and many substantial institutions have become a part of huge holding companies which may own all or the controlling stock of many associations.

In the period between 1956 and 1961, many of these holding companies "went public" and their shares attracted great followings. The California institutions, because of the intense regional demand for home mortgage funds (stimulated by the rapid population increase in California), became very profitable. They attracted hundreds of millions of savers' dollars from the East by above-average interest rates; and in turn loaned money on mortgages at much higher rates than those prevailing on the Eastern Seaboard. Some institutions in 1959-61 were operating on a gross "spread" of as much as 2 percent between the rate they paid to savers and the rates received from borrowers. As a result, S&L shares in 1961 became market darlings, with Great Western Financial hitting a high of 62 1/2.

Then came the turnabout: Eastern banks and S&L's began to pay higher rates on savings accounts, and demand for mortgage money in California began to slacken. Profit margins for S&L's dwindled, and there was a tendency in certain institutions to lower lending standards in order to make loans paying higher interest rates. By 1965, many of these unwise, or marginal, loans went bad, and several S&L companies had "scheduled" loans (behind in interest or principal payments) to as much as 10 percent of their portfolios. Nonpaying mortgages reduce the flow of income to an association, and there were, in the 1965 reports, many severe declines in earnings; and low earnings persisted through 1966. As a result, many S&L shares plummeted in 1965-66, selling, at their lows, sometimes 80 percent below their 1961 highs.

All this financial unpleasantness created a situation in late 1966 wherein many S&L shares seemed unduly depressed. An improvement in lending, a renewed demand for housing, rising real-estate prices, renewed flow of savers' funds, and the "working out" of a high percentage of scheduled items suggest that S&L stocks generally may stage a notable comeback in 1967, and we feel rather confident about three issues.

GREAT WESTERN FINANCIAL

This is the second largest S&L holding company. It earned $1.23 on its common stock in 1965 and about 75 cents in 1966. Great Western now appears headed up again. It may earn $1.20 in 1967 and $1.75 in 1968. Its scheduled items in autumn, 1966, were around 5.4 percent, and the company has deemphasized construction loans and housing-development loans (more volatile in quality but usually carrying high interest rates).

There are 8,589,000 shares of Great Western listed on NYSE, selling on January 11, 1967, at 12. The 1966 low was 5 3/4, and the 1961 high was 62 1/2. This issue may now be on the way up again, and could, we think, hit 24 in 1967.

FIRST CHARTER FINANCIAL

This company has enjoyed the reputation for top management and investment quality in the S&L group. For some years, First Charter was more farsighted and prudent in its lending than some of its competitors, and its scheduled items in 1966 were very low — around 4 percent. Moreover, with units located in northern California, the company has generated its savings mostly in-state and has paid savers consistently higher interest than the commercial banks, with which it competes. (There are no mutual savings banks in California.)

It is our feeling that First Charter Financial is a top-quality institution. Earnings on 8,944,000 shares of common at around $1.20 per share for 1966 could expand by at least 50 percent in 1967 and reach $2.75 or better in 1968. On this assumption, we can envision FCF common as a $40 stock by Christmas, with a great assist from impetuous speculators. Many shrewd old traders, operating in a recovery industry, insist on buying the top-rated stock within it. FCF would rate thus. Listed on NYSE the common stock sold at 22 on January 11, 1967.

FINANCIAL FEDERATION

This distinguished holding company for eleven operating associations had a dreary year in 1966, reporting a deficit against $2.37 a share in 1965. At September 30, 1966, total scheduled assets were about 12 percent of portfolio, and it will require time and a more buoyant realty market to work down this list of delinquent portfolio items.

Financial Federation is a very large institution (third in California), with total assets of $1.15 billion. Book value, as of September 30, 1966, was $25.74. A rather compact capitalization of only 2,720,149 shares gives FFI a lot of leverage, augmented by combined notes payable and Federal Home Loan Bank advances (also at September 30, 1966) of about $185 million. FFI sold at 91 1/8 in 1961 and as low as 8 1/2 in 1966. At its January, 1967, price of 17 5/8, the company could advance briskly to $35 or more if earnings recover with some vigor.

19

possible doublers: assorted speculations of promise

In the past three chapters, we highlighted certain security speculations that appeared promising due to the favorable 1967 prospects of particular industries — life insurance, savings and loan, and oil. In this chapter, however, we present a group of speculations selected from everywhere. Each one is believed to possess certain qualities that may hopefully cause it to outperform the market by a wide margin. We shall, moreover, conclude this chapter with a complete list of all the stocks we have selected for possible stellar market performance in 1967, including a "second team" list.

BAUSCH & LOMB, INC.

Here's a scientific company with vision! It is the second largest optical company in the United States. It makes spectacles, lenses, mountings, and frames, and enjoys a global reputation for product excellence and advance design of its optical and scientific equipment for research and for medical, industrial, educational, and military use.

About 50 percent of company sales come from its ophthalmic division. This is a bread-and-butter business but growing rapidly to serve the 91 million Americans who wear glasses, of whom at least 45 million require further eye care. BOL also makes its Ray-Ban line of sunglasses, which excel in fashion and function.

The company has recorded noted breakthroughs in plastic lenses and in contact lenses of hydrophilic polymer. Bausch & Lomb is also a leader among the makers of professional ophthalmic instruments.

The scientific instrument division accounts for about 40 percent of sales. Products here include microscopes, laser projectors, lenses for cameras, holographic equipment, spectrophotometers, log linear recorders, and the like. This division draws on one hundred years of optical knowledge and skill to supply data-processing-

and-collection systems with instruments and equipment for translation of visible data into electrical impulses. Growth here is also expected in infrared technology, optical scanners, and missile-guidance and tracking systems.

About 2,061,448 shares of common are listed for trading on NYSE. The January price was 62. The issue seems to be steadily under accumulation. While it sells at a high price related to a 1966 per share net of around $2.75, it's an elite equity, combining quality, research excellence, and fine cost controls, with scarcity. It could attract the kind of high-level speculative following associated with Corning Glass, Fairchild Camera, or Polaroid. A price of 100 seems possible and 140 not incredible.

GENERAL DEVELOPMENT CORPORATION

Here is a speculation in land — originally 92,700 acres at Port Charlotte, with some 9,600 homesites, 5,200 houses, and several commercial sites sold at December 1, 1966. Port Lucie had 36,500 acres originally; Port Malabar 42,250 acres; and the company had a land spread totaling 10,000 acres in other Florida communities.

The company's procedure is to own extensive tracts of raw land; improve them with roads, and with water, sewage, and propane-gas services (which supply continuing revenues after land is sold); build and sell houses thereon; and establish appropriate community facilities — shopping centers, churches, golf clubs, hospitals.

Through some 115 sales agents and branch offices in many cities, the company sells home-sites for as little as $25 down and $20 monthly; and also completed houses.

General Development stands to benefit from gains in net worth, as realty prices advance over the years, and as improvements cause the remaining unsold land and, later, built houses, to command substantially greater market prices.

Per-share earnings are unimpressive and sales, running around $32 million a year, are well below the $68.4 million in sales reported in 1961. The potentials for enhanced land value, rising earnings from, and possible gainful sale of, utilities built to serve new communities, all point to this stock as a valid speculation in an inflationary economy.

There are 7,529,640 shares of common outstanding, about one-third closely held. City Investing Company, a notably successful realty enterprise, purchased 242,702 shares in the spring of 1966. Shares sold at 30 1/8 in 1959. It should start heading back in that direction in 1967, possibly to $14 or $15. Quotation on January 11, 1967: 6 1/4 on NYSE. The stock could move, because they're still making people but they've stopped making land!

GREATAMERICA CORPORATION

This is a sizable holding company and a special-situation type of stock. Balance-sheet value of company assets at December 31, 1965, was $258.8 million against an indicated market

value of over $500 million. A gifted manage-
ment, headed by Mr. Troy V. Post, Chairman,
has shepherded substantial investments in growing companies. Investment holdings include
81 percent of Braniff Airways common, 57 percent of American-Amicable Life Insurance Company, 99 percent of First Western Bank and
Trust Company, and 7 percent of Franklin Life
Insurance Company.

During 1966, Greatamerica arranged the sale
of 3,199,660 shares (retaining 1,219,215 shares)
of its Franklin Life stock at $30 a share to Con-
tinental Insurance Company, realizing around
$96 million in cash. Much of this money is ex-
pected to be reinvested in Braniff Airways. This
is a major air-transport trunkline (including
Panagra, recently purchased for $30 million)
serving the central United States and strategic
South American routes. In the past two years,
gross revenues and net earnings have moved
ahead rapidly. Greatamerica's fortunes are
geared importantly to Braniff, its largest single
investment.

If you allow for adjusted earnings of its insurance holdings, net earnings for 1966 were
probably above $1 a share on the 15,674,317
common shares outstanding. Greatamerica common traded OTC and was quoted (January 11,
1967) at 15 3/8. The combination of airline and
financial companies, the traditional sagacity of
management, and the breadth of market interest
in, and sponsorship of, this issue point to possible market virtuosity in 1967 and maybe a price
close to $40.

AUTOMATIC SPRINKLER CORPORATION
OF AMERICA

Automatic Sprinkler Corporation of America is a vigorous company, rapidly expanding by a series of acquisitions. It is an important manufacturer of automatic-fire-sprinkler systems, portable fire extinguishers, hoses, nozzles, fire engines, battery-driven mining vehicles, tubular products, pipe fittings, and hangars; and is a distributor of tires and batteries.

Rapid acquisitions of companies (including, in 1966, American LaFrance and Safeway Steel Products, maker of steel scaffolds, towers, bleachers for sporting arenas and stadiums) make rather incomplete a current definition of gross sales. Sales did, however, increase from $25 million in 1964 to over $45 million in 1965, accompanied by a 75 percent rise in net earnings per share.

Common stock, as of November 1, 1966, was outstanding in the amount of 3,281,272 shares (10 cents par) and preceded by $5.6 million in long debt and $6.2 million par amount of preferred stock. A majority of common is believed closely held.

Confidence in the speculative potentials of Automatic Sprinkler stems from the reputation of the company for quality products since 1910; shrewd acquisition and efficient assimilation of profitable companies fitting in well with existing patterns of manufacturing and marketing; and the dynamic growth in the market for fire-fighting and prevention equipment. Possibly, too, the company's line of battery-propelled cars and tractors may be expanded in an air-pollution-minded world.

Publicly offered at $19.50 a share in November, 1965, common was quoted at 27 1/4 OTC on January 11, 1967. If this issue continues to gain market sponsorship, it may become a performer, and possible doubler, in 1967.

MILLIPORE CORPORATION

Here's a sporting speculation in a company researching and producing membrane filters and sophisticated instruments and equipment for control or removal of microscopic particles or elements from liquids or gases. The best-known Millipore breakthrough is its filtration method for delivery of draft beer in cans without deterioration in its quality, flavor, or condition.

End uses of Millipore filters are in the sterilizing of drugs and vaccines; in the filtering out of bacteria in soft drinks (as well as beer); and in a process for displacing pasteurization, by destroying bacteria without affecting taste, texture, or chemical composition of fluids. The company also manufactures and markets laboratory equipment, accessories for pumps, electronic monitors, and microscopes for use with filters and filter systems.

Sales have moved rapidly ahead from $4.5 million in 1964 to $6.28 million in 1965 and probably around $9 million in 1966. For the nine months ending September 30, 1966, net income was 78 cents a share (on a larger number of shares), contrasted with thirty-three cents in the comparable 1965 period. There are 1,724,007 shares outstanding, trading OTC at 36.

Millipore common is special unto itself. Its filters, some as minute as 10 million microns, may find constantly broadened use in science, medicine, and the purification and preservation of foods and fluids. If so, the stock may romp after the manner of Kalvar, Itek, or Recognition Equipment. In that event, it could easily double from 36 (56,000 shares were offered as a secondary in the spring of 1966 at $33.75). Book value of around $9.50 is no clue to the romance in this one.

IOWA BEEF PACKERS

This stock has been a real swinger, ranging in 1966 between 18 3/4 and 68 1/2. The reason for speculative zeal here is the remarkable efficiency of company plants and their swift accommodation to changes in slaughtering schedules. The company has two beef-packing plants in Iowa and one at Dakota City, Nebraska. It also does an extensive cattle-feeding business and processes such by-products as hides and tallows. Sioux Quality Packers was acquired on October 28, 1966.

Iowa Beef Packers, located in the heart of America's major feeding regions, is a huge operation, as indicated by its sales of $426 million for the year ending October 31, 1966 (up from $289 million in fiscal 1965). Although net income of but $3 million was reported for fiscal 1966, results were affected by strikes at two plants, costing seventy-six work days. The big potential here is the tremendous leverage that improved profit margins may create per common share. There are about 2 million common shares outstanding quoted at 34 1/4, preceded by $14.4 million in long-term debt. Just 1 percent improvement in net profit margin converts to $2 a share on Iowa Packers common.

With a good packing year, no strikes, and favorable meat prices, this stock could zoom. It is best described as leverage on the hoof. It may double in 1967 and bring home the bacon!

CARTER-WALLACE, INC.

Here is a special situation — a turnaround one. The company has been in a rather languid posture due to Food and Drug Administration hearings on Carter's patented meprobamate drug. Carter markets this itself as Miltown, but under a court consent decree, must sell it in bulk at $20 a pound to other properly qualified pharmaceutical firms (without discrimination).

Wallace Laboratories is the ethical-drug division, producing not only Miltown, but Milpath for intestinal disorders; Appetrol to cut down appetite; Miltrate for angina; Soma for relaxed muscles; and Solacen, an antineurotic drug.

In toiletries, the company makes and markets Arrid in cream and spray; Rise, an aerosol-type shave cream; and Nair, for removing excess hair, all among the leaders in their fields. Then there are, of course, the famous Carter's Little Pills, a renowned proprietary item. Carter also has a 44 percent interest in a drug-chemical maker, Millmaster Onyx Corporation; and, in 1962, bought for cash all but 7 percent of the stock in Frank W. Horner, Ltd., a Canadian maker and marketer of vitamins and antibiotics.

Earnings have been on a plateau around $1.50 per share for a couple of years, and the stock became neglected by speculators and was sold out by some institutions. Now, however, a turn-around seems possible. The FDA outcome may be less disturbing than assumed, earnings look upward, and the company is well situated with cash resources for the right acquisitions. Further, Carter-Wallace is planning to embark on significant new product activity in women's and men's toiletries. This stock, selling as low as 10 1/8 in 1966, has plenty of rebound potentials from 14 1/4. It could surprise speculators and delight its 6,300 stockholders by moving up spryly. More than half the 7.5 million common shares are very closely held, leaving about 3.5 million tradable. There is no long-term debt.

H. C. BOHACK COMPANY

Here's another special situation — an old and honored food chain of 195 stores principally in Brooklyn and on Long Island, with annual sales of over $200 million but operating losses for the past two years. In the October, 1966, quarter, however, there was a turnabout and a small profit materialized. Management changes, plus renovation of major supermarkets and dropping some outmoded and unprofitable units, would seem to place Bohack in a position to do better. The company has extensive facilities, including a huge warehouse with large refrigeration, packing, and coffee-roasting facilities.

The leverage here is supplied by the existence of only 497,276 common shares, preceded by $4.2 million par value of $5.50 preferred, $1 million in minority interest, and $11.2 million in long-term debt. A profit margin of just 1 percent on sales would produce $4 a share in net on the common. This is a speculation, but not too wild a one at 14 3/4. The stock sold above 40 in 1961!

WATSCO, INC.

Here's a lively young company formed in April, 1961, by a merger of Wagner Tool & Supply Corporation and Devices Research Corporation; and supplemented by acquisition, October 21, 1963, of Acme Plating and Finishing Corporation. Watsco's primary business is the manufacture and marketing of control and check valves, metering devices, and terminal seals used for refrigerant controls in air-conditioning and refrigerating systems. The dynamic uptrend in installation of air-conditioning in homes, offices, industrial and institutional structures has been a major factor in company growth.

Corporate horizons were broadened when, on April 1, 1964, Winslow Manufacturing Corporation was acquired by Watsco, Inc. Winslow manufactures a professional hair-spraying system for beauty salons and beauty-culture schools, plus a line of lacquers, sprays, sets, and shampoos used in conjunction with the hair-spray system. Winslow equipment is now located in over 25,000 beauty salons. Watsco's plant for its own and Winslow products is at Hialeah, Florida.

For nine months ending October 31, 1966, consolidated sales were $1,845,169, and distilled into $297,093 net after taxes. After a 100 percent stock dividend on July 20, 1966, there are outstanding approximately 683,894 shares of common stock (trading OTC), preceded by about $1,700,000 in debt securities. Indications point to a per share net of 80 cents plus in 1967 and suggest that Watsco common at $5 a share may be substantially undervalued. Watsco is a young company. If it continues to grow at the same rate in the next five years as in the past, it should perform well marketwise. A speculation, to be sure, but one that could double. Earnings have been retained by meager cash dividends (4 cents a share quarterly) supplemented by stock dividends. If the company continues to grow at the present rate, it might qualify for ASE listing in 1967.

BRAZILIAN LIGHT & POWER COMPANY

Here is a remarkable speculation. It could double this year. A highly solvent utility company and the largest company in Brazil, it languishes for only one reason — political and economic uncertainty in the largest South American republic.

This Canadian holding company serves some of the most important cities and areas of Brazil — Rio de Janeiro, Sao Paulo, and Santos — with electricity and gas. Its plants stand on the books at over $1 billion and could not be duplicated today for less than $2 billion. Net per share of around $1.20 in 1966 permitted dividend payments of $1 a share.

There are 17,294,671 shares of ordinary (common) stock outstanding, listed on the American Stock Exchange. At a current price around $9.75 per share, the issue provides (on the $1 dividend) a remarkable yield for a speculative security. Achievement of economic equilibrium in Brazil and stabilizing of its currency might result in notable market gain for this special-situation equity. Reportedly, 1 million or more shares are held by International Mining Corporation. Book value is over $30 a share! Between low and high prices for each year, this stock doubled in 1961, 1962, 1963, 1964, and 1965. It might encore in 1967.

SHERATON CORPORATION

Here the speculative appeal is in real estate. Through subsidiaries, Sheraton operates or franchises about 122 hotels and motels. Most are in the United States and owned and operated under the Sheraton name. Their biggest recent expansion has been in motor inns in America and construction of new hotels abroad — in Kuwait,

Manila, Cairo, Beirut, Malta, and Aruba. Some commercial properties, an 87 percent interest in Thomson Industries, a metal stamping company, and a 3 percent interest in Diners Club Inc., provide measures of diversification.

The hotel operations deliver three-fourths of the annual gross revenues; but Sheraton has increased its net per share in many years by sale of properties for capital gain (58 cents in 1965). In an inflationary economy, the 5,546,786 common shares listed on the NYSE might well advance above the January 11 price of 10 1/2.

KAISER INDUSTRIES

This is a composite company. In operations it includes the Jeep Corporation, producer of utility vehicles, station wagons, and military motor units under the renowned "Jeep" name. Other operating subsidiaries include an engineering and construction business, a sand and gravel company, and Kaiser Aerospace & Electronics.

KI is also a substantial investment company, owning stock interests of 50 percent or more in Kaiser Steel, National Steel and Shipbuilding, and Kaiser Community Homes; 41 percent of Kaiser Aluminum, and 39 percent of Kaiser Cement and Gypsum. At September 30, 1966, market value of security holdings was about twice book value.

Kaiser Industries does not impress one on past earnings, and the company had a tax loss carry forward of about $25 million at January 1, 1966. Against a loss in 1965, the company reported a modest profit in 1966. The big hope for gain here, however, is potential rise in securities held. There are some good companies in this group, and major gains in this issue are possible in a strong market. The January 11 price was 11 3/4. There are 22,912,391 common shares outstanding, 61 percent held by the Kaiser family.

RHEINGOLD CORPORATION

This is a beverage company with a bright future. Its Rheingold Breweries sell in eleven states, and it acquired the rights to Ruppert Knickerbocker Beer in late 1965. Combining these two brewing operations, Rheingold is thought to be the eleventh largest brewer in America. The company has as well import rights for Tuborg Beer.

In addition, Rheingold Corporation is the largest independent bottler of Pepsi-Cola with operating, bottling, and marketing facilities in Los Angeles, Puerto Rico, and Mexico.

Earnings have shown a strong growth, rising from $1.15 per share in 1964 to $1.45 in 1965 and $1.70 in 1966. There are 2,962,690 common shares outstanding, preceded by $34.5 million in long debt. Situated in a strong consumer market, and benefiting from energetic management, RG might become a market favorite in 1967 — and double. Starting price is 19.

LIST I

TABULATION OF
SELECTED DESCRIBED SPECULATIONS

ISSUE	TRADED	PRICE JAN. 11, 1967
Bausch & Lomb	(NYSE)	62
General Development Corporation	(NYSE)	6 1/4
Greatamerica Corporation	(OTC)	15 1/4
Automatic Sprinkler	(OTC)	27 1/8
Millipore Corporation	(OTC)	36
Iowa Beef Packers	(OTC)	34 1/4
Carter-Wallace	(NYSE)	14 1/4
H. C. Bohack Company	(ASE)	14 3/4
Watsco, Inc.	(OTC)	5 3/4
Brazilian Light & Power Company	(ASE)	10
Sheraton Corporation	(NYSE)	10 1/2
Rheingold Corporation	(NYSE)	19
Kaiser Industries	(ASE)	11 3/4
Life Insurance Company of Kentucky	(OTC)	20 7/8
Liberty Life Insurance Company	(OTC)	20 3/4
National Investors Life Insurance Company	(OTC)	7 1/2
Santa Fe Drilling Company	(NYSE)	29 1/8
Global Marine	(OTC)	30 1/2
Canadian Superior Oil Ltd.	(ASE)	29 7/8
Provo Gas Producers Ltd.	(Toronto)	5.60
Central-Del Rio Oils Ltd.	(Toronto)	13.25
Canadian Export Gas & Oil	(ASE)	4 7/8
Great Western Financial	(NYSE)	12
First Charter Financial	(NYSE)	22
Financial Federation	(NYSE)	17 5/8

LIST II

FURTHER STOCKS
WITH VARYING ELEMENTS OF VOLATILITY

ISSUE	PRICE JAN. 11, 1967
Norfolk Southern Railway (ASE)	40 3/4
Strategic Virginia and North Carolina railroad with merger potentials.	
Canadian Homestead Oil (ASE)	2 1/4
Petroleum producer with low price and high hopes.	
Alleghany Corporation Warrants (ASE)	6 1/2
Leveraged call on a lively investment company.	
Solon Automated Services, Inc. (OTC)	4 1/2
Coin-operated laundry equipment.	
United Life and Accident Company (OTC)	12 1/2
Excellent management, highly leveraged Life company in Concord, New Hampshire.	
Detrex Chemical (OTC)	18
A tritetrachlorine maker plus machines to make it. Nineteen-year dividend record and a steep upturn in earnings.	
Kennametal (NYSE)	40
Sophisticated metals for the space age.	
Kentucky Fried Chicken Corporation (OTC)	30 1/2
Very fast growing and well-managed convenience take-home food company.	
Lewis Business Form (OTC)	25 1/2
Paper forms and cards to service the computer and data-processing age.	
Recognition Equipment (OTC)	64
Could be a swinger like Kalvar, ITEK, Solitron. Risk and volatility on the hoof.	
University Computers (OTC)	28
Leases computers.	
Univis Inc. (OTC)	20
Eyeglasses and mergers.	

ISSUE	PRICE JAN. 11, 1967
Cubic Corporation (ASE) An electronic age swinger that could swing again.	12 3/4
Alaska Air Line (ASE) Rapidly growing air transport company with rising earnings.	11
Brown Company (NYSE) Owns a broad swath of timber land, has energetic management and upswing in earnings.	18
Maust Coal (OTC) May bound back from a depressing 1966.	9
Arvida Corporation (OTC) Florida land awaiting development and demand.	6
McLean Industries (OTC) Down from 54.	17
Data Processing Financial and General (ASE) Computer leasing, plus gifted management.	52 1/8
Scurry Rainbow Oil (ASE) Oil and potash in Alberta.	19 3/4

20
the roundup

In earlier chapters, we have tabulated market doublers over a six-year period and have presented a screened list of equities with, presumably, above-average propensity to double in 1967. We have by no means, however, covered the entire market arena. We didn't say much about Canadian markets on account of the 15 percent equalization tax, and we didn't summarize OTC results.

THE OVER-THE-COUNTER MARKET

Existing side by side with American listed issues are some 7,500 stocks that trade, or are quoted, with some regularity over-the-counter. The OTC market is in fact the world's largest one, although it suffers from want of publicity and trader popularity. There is no official record of sales volumes, actual prices at which transactions are made, or price swings, on any business day. Further, many unlisted companies fail to supply as complete or as regular corporate financial reports as are required for stocks listed on ASE or NYSE.

PREFERENCE FOR LISTING

If you look over almost any list of stocks recommended by a substantial brokerage firm, you will note that most of the issues are listed on the American or New York Stock Exchange. Listed issues generally: (1) are the equities of larger, better known companies, (2) are seasoned, (3) are outstanding in larger amounts, (4) trade in greater daily volume, (5) are preferred by institutional investors, and (6) are more acceptable collateral for loan purposes. A final reason for investor preference of listed (versus OTC) issues is breadth of market. If you wish to buy, say, 1,000 shares of stock, you are, in most cases, much more likely to have the order executed promptly, and without any significant change from the last price quotation, on an exchange than OTC. Since traders seek swift action, they naturally prefer issues with broad, active markets where orders can be executed immediately. In selling or buying several hundred shares of a stock over-the-counter, it is, on occasion, necessary to wait for several hours, and to check the market in several places before the order can be completed at an acceptable price.

OTC STOCKS

Just because unlisted issues are generally less publicized and less active is no reason, however, to ignore or neglect the OTC market. Far more issues in this market sector double each year than do stocks on the exchanges; and, in many cases, price swings are more dramatic. For example, Airlift International common sold in December, 1966, at 50 cents. Yet it advanced to over $5 a share in January, 1967. Kalvar zoomed from 41 in December, 1966, to 180 in early February, 1967, yet this company has lost money each year for more than a decade!

Most investors regard the OTC market as the habitat of smaller, lesser known stocks, low in price and investment quality; and of newer and riskier issues. It is true that hundreds of OTC stocks fall into these categories. It is also true, however, that some of the finest equities in the world trade OTC and nowhere else. There are, for example, about fourteen thousand commercial banks in the United States.

The stocks of all of these (unless closely or family-held), with the single exception of Chase Manhattan (listed NYSE), trade over-the-counter. The shares in the fifteen hundred stock life insurance companies *all* trade OTC. So do many fire and casualty company shares, most preferred stocks, all open-end mutual funds, 95 percent of all government bonds, most municipal bonds, and dozens of issues of corporation bonds. If you wish to buy such quality stocks as Morgan Guaranty Trust, Aetna Life Insurance, Bank of America, American Express, Anheuser-Busch, Grinnell Corporation, Eli Lilly, The New Yorker, you buy them OTC.

All new issues start out trading over-the-counter, even though they may move to listed status later on; and each year there is a steady migration of dozens of issues from the OTC market to exchange listing. On occasion, vigorous price swings may take place, OTC, in issues about to become listed. In June, 1964, Comsat came out at $20. After trading actively OTC to a high of $48, it was listed on NYSE on September 8, 1964; and reached a listed high in that year of 71 1/2. Comsat is a stock that doubled in a year, although it does not appear in one of the lists of doublers since its gains were split between over-the-counter and exchange trading.

All of the above is to suggest to you that you not neglect OTC stocks even though most of the issues you may acquire for short-run speculative gains are listed ones. Stocks such as Kalvar,

Recognition Equipment, Permeator Corporation, Kentucky Fried Chicken, active life stocks, electronic and scientific issues can move dramatically OTC; and many newer, lower priced issues often develop lively market flurries in response to exciting corporate developments. Thin markets and scarcity are often important factors in OTC trading swings.

Perhaps the liveliest OTC market activity occurs when new issues are brought out. In a bullish financial year, over a billion dollars in new stock issues may be underwritten by investment banking firms, brokers, and dealers across the land. There is no conclusive performance trend among these. Some go up immediately, some go down, and others just meander along at around their issue price, without attracting any significant speculative interest. You should, however, always keep your eyes open for a potentially "hot" new issue. Some of them reward their early buyers well, and in a hurry! To illustrate, of the dozens of new stock offerings in 1966 — a downtrend market year — Kentucky Fried Chicken common came out at $15 and closed the year at $31; Medicenters of America was offered at 10 and closed at 20 1/4; Riker Video Industries moved from 7 1/2 to 19; and Tridair Industries, from 16 to 32 1/2. This represents a rather small percentage of winners out of over one hundred new offerings, but it illustrates the rapid gains possible if you are lucky enough to buy the right ones.

Had we reviewed all OTC issues, new and old, trading in the OTC arena 1961-66, this book would have become a mass of tables and a rather arid statistical summary. Further, for most active market traders, in search of short-term gains, listed issues in a majority of cases will provide greater market mobility, generate a more numerous and aggressive market following, and benefit from the propelling force of institutional buying. It must ever be borne in mind that when you buy a stock for gain, you will want somebody on hand to buy it from you at a higher price later on. That is why you should stress issues that have, or can generate, eager market sponsorship — to assure that there will be avid buyers around when you decide to sell. It is the breadth and activity of listed markets that generally make them preferable for short-term speculation, although growth-minded investors can often reap not 100 percent but several hundred percent profits by prudent selection and patient retention (for several years) of properly researched OTC issues. Life shares are notable examples of this.

SUMMARY AND CONCLUSION

We are now drawing to the close of *Happiness Is a Stock That Doubles in a Year*. It is a rather unconventional book, based on the premise that, with luck, you can select in advance issues with notable potentials for swift gain and that such issues often have common characteristics. In a way, it is also a practical book, because it seeks to select for future profits issues resembling or comparable to stocks that have actually doubled in previous years.

NO WARRANTY OFFERED

Bear in mind that in the stock market there are no real experts, just a few gifted artists, because investment is still far more an art than a science. Also, do not expect too much of your author! He is by profession neither a magician nor a soothsayer. He is an economist, an eager follower of security markets for more than forty years, and an avid and voracious reader of financial literature written by men just as knowledgeable and resourceful as he is. From these men, many of whom are brilliant and successful traders, he has gleaned certain ideas, methods, and techniques for security selection and stock trading that have in the past produced rewarding results — for them! May they do as well for you! But remember, anybody who guarantees a profit in the stock market is a fool or a charlatan. This book makes no guarantees.

The most important thing to keep in mind in trading stocks for gain is that, among the best and worst stocks, price swings in both directions can be swift, unreasonable, and unpredictable; and you must be as willing to sell at the proper time as you were to buy.

WHEN TO SELL

Since most of what we have talked about concerns when and how to buy stocks that may go up, we should conclude with a few pertinent observations on when and how to sell. So here they are.

You should sell your trading stocks, hopefully, at a price near the objective you have set. In this book, this price is defined as 100 percent over cost. Obviously, this is arbitrary and many stocks may not prove that accommodating! They may stubbornly rise 80 percent, 40 percent — or not at all — and then just sit there!

Here are some sensible guidelines as to when to sell what stocks, in those instances where a 100 percent gain does not seem about to materialize.

The times to sell stock are:

1. When you need the cash.

2. When the whole market appears too high or has stopped rising.

3. When shares in a particular industry get gaudily overpriced — above 55 times earnings.

4. When earnings on a particular stock are heading downward (for at least two quarters).

5. When stocks yield 1.5 percent below quality bonds.

6. When fewer and fewer issues make new highs.

7. When "the clamor of bulls is loudest."

8. When a given stock has attained the price objective for which you bought it.

Don't hesitate to sell when there are powerful indications that you should do so. And when
you sell, don't go shopping for "eighths." Sell
at the market.

DIVERSIFICATION

We should at least mention diversification,
since it is one of the most time-honored prin-
ciples of prudent investment. In seeking success in market trading, however, forget it! You're
depending for gain not on the law of averages
but on screened selection of issues that can far
outperform the average — and the averages!
From the array of gainful hopefuls we have
gathered together, pick just five! Pick the ones
you like and that you have properly verified and
checked on with a competent broker or financial
service journal. The issues you actually buy
need not be any of the ones we've mentioned.
You may select others with similar aggressive
characteristics that you've dug up yourself or
had recommended to you. We'd be silly indeed
to assert that among some thirty-four thousand
readily marketable issues, we have come upon
the only ones that have a chance to double in
1967. In any event, however, stick to five stocks
unless you're entering the market with $100,000
or more; then you can work with eight or ten
tops. Select — don't scatter your holdings.

INFLATION

No one talks about stocks these days without reference to inflation. While our cost of living has gone up about 60 percent since the end of World War II, we haven't really had a roaring inflation — such as they experience regularly in Argentina. There, prices were up 40 percent in 1966, and the currency was revaluated twice. At the rate we're going, however, we may get some heavier doses of inflation here, possibly in 1967 but surely by 1970. Everything points to it: an inexorable increase in the price of labor; the cost of government; and the levels of personal, municipal, government, and corporate debt. Inflation is the classic device by which debtors get "off the hook."

If and when we do get a dose of inflation, then certain stocks seem to offer a useful hedge. The companies to be preferred are those with very low labor costs; those rich with natural resources — oil, minerals and metals (gold, silver, copper, nickel), timber, land; and those companies that can maintain a high level of profitability by increasing their prices faster than their labor costs. These would include certain service industries and most of those companies that are highly automated or produce labor- and time-saving equipment. Land and land stocks are traditionally desirable. As we said before, we're still making people, but we've stopped making land!

RANDOM AFTERTHOUGHTS

We've referred throughout to the Dow-Jones Industrial Average as the key index or barometer of the level of stock prices. We have done so not to discriminate against other indices but because the DJIA is indeed an effective market altimeter. The list of thirty issues, given earlier, represents a good cross section of the largest companies in America; and this average has been kept for so many years that it is valid for making comparisons of trends, ranges, and altitudes. There are, of course, a lot of others you may refer to if you choose: the Standard & Poor's Index of 425 industrials; *The New York Times* list of 100 stocks; and more recently the composite indices of both the New York Stock Exchange and the American Stock Exchange. All of these are more stable than DJIA; but our primary interest is obviously in market velocity and volatility, not stability.

THE IMPOSSIBLE DREAM

Finally, this book is just a little psychedelic. It offers to launch you into a dream world of equities that offer the phantom of a performance far better than 95 percent of all other traded issues. This is an incredible objective and just a little far out. The book should actually be read to the accompaniment of the hit song from *Man of La Mancha*, called "To Dream the Impossible Dream." However, the attainment of any goal, no matter how remote, demands that you first have the goal in mind. There is no absolutely perpendicular building, yet if a plumb line were not used, most structures would resemble the Tower of Pisa. No golfer breaks par unless he tries to, and unless he develops the necessary skill, confidence, and courage. So it is with the stock market. Only a few will actually double their money in any year—and those who do will have concentrated on their task. Concentrate and get lucky, and you may indeed discover that *happiness is a stock that doubles in a year.* But please always remember one thing: This book is a road map, not an insurance policy!

index

ABOUT THE AUTHOR

IRA U. COBLEIGH is an economist who for the past seventeen years has been the feature and financial editor of *The Commercial and Financial Chronicle*. He is vice-president and economist of the DeWitt, Conklin Organization, Inc., a financial communications firm, and a director of five corporations. He is the author of a number of books that have sold, in total, over one million copies, including *Guide to Success in the Stock Market, How to Gain Security and Financial Independence, Expanding Your Income, Life Insurance for Financial Gains, 100 Billion Dollars Can't Be Wrong*. A graduate of Columbia College, Mr. Cobleigh lives on Long Island with his wife, Dorothy. They have two sons and three grandchildren.